LYING, CHEATING, STEALING

D1003259

CRIMINAL CAREERS

Volume One
EXPLAINING CRIMINALS

Volume Two
KILLING ONE ANOTHER

Volume Three
LYING, CHEATING, STEALING

Volume Four
RESPONDING TO CRIME

LYING, CHEATING, STEALING

GWYNN NETTLER

Professor Emeritus of Sociology
University of Alberta
Edmonton, Canada

CRIMINAL CAREERS VOLUME THREE
Anderson Publishing Co. / Cincinnati, Ohio

Rick Adams, Publisher's Staff Editor

CRIMINAL CAREERS VOLUME THREE: LYING, CHEATING, STEALING

Library of Congress Cataloging in Publication Data
Nettler, Gwynn.
    Lying, cheating, stealing.

    (Criminal careers ; v. 3)
    Bibliography: p.
    Includes indexes.
    1. Fraud. 2. Stealing. 3. Treason. I. Title.
II. Series: Nettler, Gwynn. Criminal careers ; v. 3.
HV6691.N47   364.1'62   81–70992
ISBN 0–87084–602–7   AACR2

Second Printing – August 1988

Designed by William A. Burden

 Criminal Justice Studies
Anderson Publishing Co./Cincinnati, Ohio

John L. Mason, President   Jean C. Martin, Executive Editor

CONTENTS OF CRIMINAL CAREERS

Volume One   EXPLAINING CRIMINALS
             Themes
  Chapter 1 Interpreting Careers
          2 Questions, Answers, and Their Uses
          3 Continuities and Contingencies
          4 Tallies
             Causes
          5 Constitutions
          6 Lessons
          7 Environments
          8 Selecting Causes

Volume Two   KILLING ONE ANOTHER
  Chapter 1 Homicide: Definitions and Justifications
          2 Social Locations of Homicide: Age, Sex, Work, Wealth
          3 Social Locations of Homicide: Cultures
          4 Contingencies
          5 Homicidal Routes: Self-Defense
          6 Homicidal Routes: Love, Spurned or Spoiled
          7 Homicidal Routes: Lust
          8 Homicidal Routes: Lunacy
          9 Homicidal Routes: Psychopathy
         10 Killing for Wealth and Power
         11 Terrorism
         12 Violence and Moral Atmosphere

Volume Three   LYING, CHEATING, STEALING
  (See next page for detailed analysis of Volume Three)

Volume Four RESPONDING TO CRIME
  Chapter 1 Doing Justice
          2 Fairness in Criminal Law
          3 Incapacitating
          4 Predicting Danger
          5 Deterring
          6 Correcting Offenders
          7 Prescriptions

DETAILED ANALYSIS OF VOLUME THREE

Preface   *x*
Acknowledgements   *xi*

Chapter 1   QUALITIES OF INJURY
  Dimensions of Injury   *4*
    Psychological Harm   *4*
    Injury to Social Security   *4*
    Injury to Social Welfare   *5*
      White-Collar Crime   *5*
    Attacks on Property   *7*
      Culture-binding   *9*
  Dishonesty   *9*
    Implications   *10*
      To lie is to intend to deceive   *10*
      To tell a lie requires a conception of truth   *11*
      Lying serves political functions   *11*
    1. Generality of Honesty   *13*
    2. Differential Distribution of Dishonesty   *14*
      Table 1.1 Distribution of Cheating Ratios Among School Children   *15*
      Belson and Associates' Study   *16*
      Table 1.2 Percentage of Boys Who Have Ever Committed Certain Thefts, Graded by Level of Seriousness   *16*
      Other Controlled Observations   *17*
      Conclusion   *18*
      Contingencies   *19*
    3. Detecting Deceit   *23*
      Procedures   *24*
    Polygraph and Voice Strain Evaluations   *26*
      The Truth Control Test (TCT)   *26*
      The Lie Control Test (LCT)   *26*
        Table 1.3 A Typical Lie Control Test   *27*
      The Guilty Knowledge Test (GKT)   *27*
      Voice Strain Assessment   *28*

Chapter 1—*Concluded*
    Validity   *28*
    Field Tests   *29*
    "Beating" the LCT   *30*
    Advice   *30*
    Uses   *31*
  Special Categories of Deceiver   *31*
    Pathological Liars   *31*
    Psychopathic Liars   *32*
    Self Deceivers   *32*
  Summary   *33*

Chapter 2   TREASON
    Deception for Good Causes   *36*
  Definitions   *37*
    Allegiance   *37*
    Content   *38*
    Accessories   *39*
    Misprision   *39*
    Punishment   *39*
    Related Crimes   *40*
      1. Sabotage   *40*
      2. Espionage   *40*
      3. Sedition   *40*
  Roads to Treason and Related Crimes   *42*
    The Main Road   *44*
      Ideology   *46*
    Impotence Lusting for Power   *47*
    Communist Ideals   *48*
      Conversion   *50*
      In Canada   *51*
      Suspects   *52*
      In France   *52*
      In Italy   *52*
      In Sweden   *52*
      In West Germany   *52*
      In Great Britain   *53*
      Bruno Pontecorvo   *53*
      The "Cambridge Four": Anthony Blunt, Guy Francis de
        Moncy Burgess, Donald Maclean, Harold Adrian Russell
        (Kim) Philby   *54*
      Climate of Treason   *55*
      In the United States   *56*
  Lessons   *58*

Chapter 3   THEFT BY FRAUD
 Costs and Benefits *62*
  Persistence of Property *62*
 Dimensions of Theft *63*
  Theft by Force *63*
  Theft by Fraud *63*
  Arson *66*
  Con-Games *68*
   Career Pleasures *71*
   Prescription *71*
  Embezzlement *71*
   A Map of One Road *71*
   Criticism *72*
   Other Roads *74*
   Competing Advice *76*
   Recent Examples *77*
  Fraud in Business and Politics *78*
 Money Motivates *80*
  Two Classic Techniques *82*
  The Ponzi *83*
  Rational Deceit *84*
  Democracy and Deceit *86*
   Propaganda as Part-Time Fraud *86*
   Governmental Ponzi *87*
   Good Intentions and Cooked Books *89*
   Another Road *91*
  Implications *91*

Chapter 4   THEFT BY FORCE AND STEALTH
 Table 4.1 Cost-Benefit Schedule for Theft *97*
 Excitement, Autonomy, Hostility *96*
  Sutton *96*
  Mesrine *99*
  Belson's Boys *101*
  Hostility *101*
 Gain *102*
  Forty-Nine Armed Robbers *102*
  Shoplifters *103*
   Boosters and Snitches *104*
  Inside Thieves *107*
  Burglary *108*

Chapter 4—*Concluded*
    Talented Thieves   *109*
        Example: MacLean   *110*
        Example: Raffles   *111*
        Vocational Hazards   *112*
    Crime and Opportunity   *112*

References   *115*

Name Index   *133*

Subject Index   *139*

PREFACE

One way to study social behavior is to think about the course of lives. All thoughtful people engage in this work, formally or informally. Journalists, novelists, and social scientists are vocationally dedicated to this task, but others who do not chart careers for a living also have opinions about what produces kinds of careers. Such opinions affect the guidance of one's own life and influence choices among public policies.

Professional students of social life have attended to segments of people's careers. These segments include childhoods, educational paths, marriages in happiness and misery, occupational shifts and continuities, and health and longevity.

The present work is in the tradition of such studies, but it attends to certain crimes as major nodes or characteristics of careers. However, the principles that inform our study have general applicability. These principles, tentatively formulated, can be applied to the interpretation of any style of life—criminal or lawful, successful, failed, or in-between. These themes provide, then, an introduction to the study of social behavior. An introduction is not a completion, of course, and our study is justified if it describes the difficulties of observing human action and of explaining it.

The text is divided into four volumes. The first part of Volume One (*Explaining Criminals*) describes interpretive themes. These are prescriptions for thinking about careers, criminal or lawful. These themes constitute assumptions that run like a thread through the substantive chapters on kinds of crime (Volume Two, *Killing One Another,* and Volume Three, *Lying, Cheating, Stealing*) and on modes of responding to crime (Volume Four, *Responding to Crime*).

The second half of Volume One develops these themes by outlining major causes of conduct. These chapters show that human action is not spun out of a simple string of causes, as it is popular to assume. On the contrary, careers are produced in a dense web of influences. A conclusion that follows is that we can know something about what the causes of conduct *can be* without knowing what they *will be* for particular individuals and particular acts.

Volume Two describes homicidal occasions. Attention is addressed to description on both aggregate and individual levels. It is emphasized that description is part of scientific explanation, but that it is not the whole of such explanation, and that there is but little science in the study of conduct.

Volume Three applies our interpretive themes in description of varieties of dishonesty, and Volume Four discusses modes of responding to crime and their justifications.

This work is intended for students of criminology, deviance, and criminal justice. It also has relevance to studies of the relations between information, knowledge, and private and public policy.

Instructors in departments of psychology and sociology, and in schools of law, criminal justice, and social work may use one volume, or all, and in any order. However, this is a book that tells a story. It reads best from beginning to end.

A booklet of discussion and test questions for each volume is available as a teaching aid. In addition, each chapter begins with an abstract that provides a study and lecture outline.

ACKNOWLEDGEMENTS

William R. Avison, Rollin C. Dudley, and Robert A. Silverman read portions of this manuscript and I thank them, and anonymous reviewers, for their suggestions. None of these readers is to blame, of course, for any of my continuing errors.

Jennefer Fraser worked with me for two years as a "detective of data." I am particularly grateful to her for her diligence and enthusiasm. I wish also to thank the editor of these volumes, Rick Adams, for his attention, imagination and editorial advice.

Gwynn Nettler

1 QUALITIES OF INJURY

Abstract • "Crime" refers to a species of wrong. Its reference moves, therefore, with moral judgment. ∘ Not all wrongs are crimes. ∘ Some crimes are not considered wrong by some citizens. • Dimensions of injury include wrongs against persons and their property. ∘ One can harm another person psychologically as well as physically. ∘ One can damage social security and social welfare as well as individuals. • The idea of "white-collar crime" refers to the possibility that respectable people may damage social welfare in the course of legitimate work. • "Property" is shown to be an extension of self. Injury to property is therefore one kind of damage to a person. ∘ Property is a conditional right, enforced by custom or law, to exlusive use of valued resources. ∘ Property excludes. Exclusivity serves a function as one resolution of "the tragedy of the commons." • Discussions of theft depend on a culturally limited conception of property. • Honesty is defined as being honorable, truthful, genuine. ∘ Dishonesty is recognized in three dimensions: Lying, cheating, and stealing. ∘ The notion of deceit rests on a conception of truth which, in turn, rests on a conception of reality. ∘ Lying is useful. It is particularly useful as an instrument with which to gain and maintain power. It is also useful as a social lubricant. • Honesty is a personality characteristic of some generality. ∘ Honesty is a more general trait than dishonesty. ∘ Characteristics of more and less honest people and contingencies of dishonesty are described. • Self-protection and social security require ability to detect deceit. ∘ Procedures for detecting deceit are described. ∘ All procedures are shown to exact a price in error for the value of some accuracy achieved. ∘ Three kinds of liars are described who may beat lie detectors: Pathological liars, psychopaths, and self-deceivers.

"CRIME" REFERS TO A SPECIES OF WRONG. The idea of crime rests, then, on moral grounds and reference of the word moves with moral judgment. There is, therefore, no essence of "criminality" to be found in an act or condition.

Legal scholars have wrestled with the notion of "crime" in an attempt to eke out a definitional victory—a victory that would indicate clearly the universal and timeless properties of a "crime" as distinct from any other disapproved act. The attempt has not been successful (Devlin 1965, Fuller 1964, Hall 1947, Hart 1965, Mitchell 1967, Smith & Hogan 1973, St. John-Stevas 1961, Williams 1958).

We are left with a legal definition of crime, the boundaries of which are constantly challenged. Legally, and briefly, crimes are intentional violations of the criminal law, pursued and punished by a state.

In culturally heterogeneous societies, challenges to legal definitions of crime are endless. Given shifting moral judgments of "wrong," demands are made simultaneously to expand and contract the scope of criminal law.

Appeals are heard to annul some old crimes and to legislate some new ones. These appeals are justified by different groups' conceptions of injury. The competing conceptions of injury refer not only to different qualities of conduct which are to be condemned officially, but also to the nature of the "victim" considered to have been damaged. Thus in all industrialized countries some crimes are those wrongs that persons commit "only"[1] upon themselves, some crimes are those that have other, particular individuals as distinct victims, and some crimes are considered to damage anonymous others referred to as "society" or "the public interest."

It is apparent, then, that not all wrongs are crimes and that, for some citizens, some crimes are not wrong. Since criminologists are *not* moral authorities,[2] they have no professional license to establish for others the proper gradient of injuries to be legislated into crimes.

[1] Injuries that persons allegedly inflict only upon themselves have been called "victim-less." For example, Schur (1965) nominates as "victim-less crimes" induced abortion, homosexuality, and drug abuse. However, right-to-life groups would not agree that induced abortion is "victim-less." So, too, depending on on one's tribe and the chemicals ingested, addiction may be considered to damage other persons than the addict. This is particularly true where addiction damages health or ability to work and the cost of dependency is passed to others. Furthermore, all groups that share a morality regard some differences in behavior as assaults upon "decency."

John Stuart Mill's famous essay *On Liberty* (1859) attempted to set limits to government intervention in our lives. To be "liberal," in this 19th century sense, was to believe that the state had no business interfering with conduct unless it "hurt" others. But, alas, no one can be a consistent "liberal" in the Millian sense because the concepts of "hurt, harm, injury" are not fixed and what is deemed to "damage" others changes. Thus Mill would not allow a person to sell his or her body in "slavery" and he wished the state to interfere when conduct offended "decency" (1859, p. 153).

Human action has no "victims" only when no one affects anyone. Definitions of "private acts" change. Thus, "If our spouses wrong *their* bodies, *we* pay a price. If children harm themselves, their parents are victims. If parents are dissolute, their children are victims. If enough individuals harm themselves, society is the victim" (Nettler 1978, p. 9, emphasis his).

[2] Some students of social behavior wish to perform as "societal engineers," deciding for others what is best for them and changing the world ac-

This needs saying for two reasons. One is that attention in these pages to particular kinds of attack and dishonesty does not deny the harm of those many other deceptions and trespasses that are *not* crimes. We damage ourselves and others in countless non-criminal ways. Attention to legally defined crimes does not invalidate those additional wrongs.

A second reason for restricting attention to crime as defined by the laws of modern states is that of time and space. No one has an inventory of all the injuries people inflict upon one another—directly and indirectly, immediately and latterly, intentionally and unintentionally. Therefore, one can nominate new crimes endlessly. For example, some sociologists have argued that differential life expectancies constitute a denial of "human rights" and that some persons or "systems" ought to be condemned as criminally responsible (Davis 1970). In this vein, H. and J. Schwendinger (1975, pp. 136–137) advocate that "imperialistic war, racism, sexism, and poverty" be made criminal. Both individuals and social systems "which cause the systematic abrogation of basic rights" are to be condemned. The Schwendingers find that:

> [H]undreds of thousands of Indo-Chinese persons are being denied the right to live; millions of black people are subjected to inhuman conditions which, on the average, deny them ten years of life; the majority of the human beings of this planet are subjected because of their sex; and an even greater number throughout the world are deprived of the commodities and services which are theirs by right. And no social system which systematically abrogates these rights is justifiable (p. 137).

Such statements are emotionally satisfying, but intellectually vacant. No one can establish by fiat what worldwide life expectancy and standard of living should be and can be. Saying this does not imply moral callousness. Rather, it recognizes *limits* to the concept of crime, to the applicability of criminal law, and to know-how in alleviation of human suffering.

---

cording to their plans. Their justification is that they "know" something and that this knowledge gives them moral authority. For example, Gouldner (1963, p. 37) asks, "If technical competence provides no warrant for making value judgments, then what does?"

As far as we can tell, the empirical answer—that is, the factual answer—is that whatever technical competence sociologists have is *not* the kind of competence most human beings *recognize* as awarding moral authority. It would make a fascinating research to ascertain how many individuals, and which ones, (a) identify a technical competence in social science; (b) of what nature; and (c) whether such recognition accords moral expertise.

DIMENSIONS OF INJURY

Criminal law identifies some kinds of attack upon persons as crimes, but the concept of a "person" includes more than an individual's body. The law also recognizes injuries to individual psyche, to social security and social welfare, and to property as wrongs against "persons." For example, Canadian criminal law says that:

> "Every one," "person," "owner," and similar expressions include Her Majesty and public bodies, bodies corporate, societies, companies, and inhabitants of counties, parishes, municipalities or other districts. . . . (Martin & Cartwright 1978, sec. 2).

Psychological Harm

As regards injury to psyche, for example, modern states recognize the crime of *libel,* the intentional defamation of another's reputation through "publication." In most countries, "publication" includes public signs or displays and televised utterance as well as printed matter. Furthermore, one can injure another's "good name" directly, or by insinuation and irony, and *without* using words (Martin & Cartwright 1978, sec. 262). Damage to a person's reputation is defined as "exposing another to hatred, contempt, or ridicule," and, in some jurisdictions, includes "publishing insults."

Another example of legal recognition of injury to psyche is the rarely prosecuted crime of *barratry.* This word derives from the Middle French term for combat and in law today it has more than one meaning. It refers to theft by fraud committed by a captain or crew of a vessel transporting others' goods, but it also refers to use of the law to harass another person. It is deemed an injury to file "excessive" and "unjust" lawsuits. For example, Marilyn Lewis was convicted in a Pittsburgh court of barratry after she had filed some 20 complaints in two years against her divorced husband, Richard (*Associated Press,* 1979). Some jurists think barratry is a "non-crime," but the present point is that the law acknowledges that one can injure others with words and litigation as well as by physical attack.

Injury to Social Security

Criminal law throughout the world also recognizes injuries to social security. Threats to social security include some of the most gravely regarded of all crimes—*treason, sabotage,* and *sedition.*

These crimes often produce physical injury and death, but the essence of treason in particular is deceit. The next chapter depicts some of the roads to treason and actors' justifications, but it is noted here as a category of crime against the public interest in which no particular individual need be identified as the victim.

Injury to Social Welfare

Laws deemed to protect social well-being run a gamut from the criminal to the regulatory. Modern states have enacted a huge library of laws and regulations justified as protective. These include laws to protect workers, consumers, the physical environment, endangered species, and special classes of people such as the young, the aged, the imprisoned, the ill, females, and selected "minorities." Many of these regulations are not codified in criminal law although they carry penalties that blur the distinction between crimes and other wrongs.

White-Collar Crime

E.H. Sutherland (1949) invented the concept of white-collar crime in order to extend the notion of criminality to those many breaches of civil and administrative law committed by corporations and by persons in business, but not ordinarily prosecuted under criminal law. Sutherland's original and persuasive thesis is that respectable citizens in commerce and industry persistently violate legislation designed to protect the public and yet are relatively immune to the stigma of criminal prosecution. He further argued that these violations damage social welfare as surely as do robbery and common larceny.

Sutherland did not intend his idea of white-collar crime to be definitive, but, rather, "to call attention to crimes which are not ordinarily included within the scope of criminology" (p. 9). He considered white-collar crime to be that "committed by a person of respectability and high social status in the course of his occupation" (p. 9).

Sutherland performed a service in attending to a broader scope of injury than that inflicted by "textbook crooks." However, government regulations have proliferated and laws have changed so rapidly in efforts to respond to a wide range of deceits, thefts, discriminatory actions, disadvantages, and other injuries that the notion of white-collar crime serves today more as a "sensitizing concept" than as a definition. Thus editors of a recent work on this tentative category of crime comment on the difficulties of definition:

> . . . we deliberately have avoided the conceptual and terminological issues involved in white-collar crime definitions. Instead, we relied on intuitively satisfying understanding of white-collar crime as a broad term

that encompasses a wide range of offenses, abuses, and crimes whose outer boundaries are as yet ill-drawn and perhaps not precisely definable (Geis & Stotland 1980, p. 1).

One can accord with the intent to study varieties of injury to persons and collectivities that are not presently addressed by the criminal law, but, at the same time, it is recognized that such study runs the risk of making "crime" an even more obscure concept than it now is. Sympathy with intent to broaden the concept of "crime" also acknowledges the following embarrassments:

1. That more laws and regulations mean more violations. New laws in particular are apt to be regarded as either unjust or as nuisances. This applies to many tax laws, including those defining income taxes.

2. That power corrupts. There is no end to "abuse" of power where "abuse" means some quality of injury as defined by individuals or interest groups. Thus, if the phrase, "white-collar crime," is to be used fairly, it deserves extension to politicians, legislators, bureaucrats, and their advisors, as well as to people in business. Then, too, depending on one's definitions of "high social status" and "course of one's occupation," white-collar crime might include idealistic, but damaging, acts of "civil disobedience."

Such extensions of the reference of "crime" will demonstrate that, as we move beyond the boundaries of traditional crimes to new ones, we quarrel about whose "abuse" ought to be termed criminal. For example, some of those who oppose the building of nuclear power plants have organized to take "direct action." Direct action against the projected Seabrook site costs the citizens of New Hampshire an estimated $750,000 for each attempted occupation of the construction zone. Citizens are now suing to recover costs from persons who use illegal tactics in exercise of their politics (*National Review* 1980).

Another example of a neglected zone of white-collar crime is that occupied by agents of governments. Bureaucrats in modern states increasingly wield irresponsible power. "Irresponsible" means that actors are not accountable for the damage they do. Tax assessors, for example, make "administrative decisions." Given the obscurity that characterizes tax law, some unknown quantity of damage is inflicted upon citizens who find it costly to contest unfair assessments.

Administrative agencies now have punitive powers which they can apply *without* due process (Simon 1978, Wallis 1976). In an illustrative case, that of *United States Department of Labor, Office of Federal Contract Compliance Programs vs. Firestone Tire and Rubber*

Company, 1980, the U.S. Secretary of Labor Ray Marshall overruled Administrative Law Judge R.J. Feldman in deciding whether Firestone was fulfilling a complicated hiring formula in its Orange, Texas, plant. The legal costs of such a dispute, and hundreds like it, are dispersed among taxpayers and, hence, difficult to identify. In addition to legal costs, commercial costs of such tangled regulations are large. In Firestone's case, the potential penalty, if the Labor Secretary's decision passes court test, is $40 million a year (*Wall Street Journal* 1980b).

In summary, broadening the concept of crime illuminates an endless array of wrongs that may be nominated for attention of the criminal law. Inspection of this array shows that all actions carry costs, that good intentions may damage innocent others as often as evil plans do, that textbook crooks are not the only agents of injury, and that there is a limit to what law can do in the control of human behavior.

Crimes, and other wrongs, that produce psychological harm, or that threaten social security and social well-being, are categories of attack upon persons. Another mode of doing harm to persons is through theft of their property.

Attacks on Property

A classic, but changing, category of injury to persons includes damage to, and expropriation of, their property. All definitions of theft rest on notions of property. But "property" is itself a word with a checkered past and an uncertain future.

The idea of property comes to us from the Latin, *propter,* a term that connotes a differential right established by custom. The customs of concern are those that determine how valued resources are to be appropriated and used. The word derives its meaning, then, from some pattern of human relations, and patterns, as we know, are subject to change. Hamilton and Till (1942, p. 530) conclude that "always and everywhere, property is an accepted medley of duties, privileges, and mutualities."

The essence of property is a conditional right, enforced by custom or law, to exclusive use of valued resources. This definition says several things:

1. However property is locally defined, the idea as applied is conditional upon conventions. This means that property rules allow exceptions and that they are subject to challenge and change.

2. The idea of property applies to a changing content of things, services, liberties, and territories.

Innovations in production, for example, change definitions of property. Thus discovery of means of communication through use of electromagnetic energy (radio and light waves) produced laws defining property in "the air waves." In North America these laws are now contested as being inefficient in the allocation of costs and as restrictive of liberty to communicate (Barrow 1975, De Vany et al. 1980, Minasian 1975).

More recently, the advent of television broadcasting by satellite has generated conflict over territorial property. Many states deem it a violation of their national sovereignty—a form of property—for another country to send signals to its people (Oettinger 1980).

Technological change is not the only source of contest about property. Shifts in the moral conception of "justice" also affect definitions of who-owns-what. For example, members of the Actors' Guild (Theater) are demanding that playwrights share their royalties with them on the ground that "there would be no plays without the actors" (Gwayne 1980). In the United States during 1979, 17 plays were blocked from rehearsal by actors on this basis. Playwrights' response to this claim to property has been to make a counter-claim against the proceeds actors receive from endorsements, TV commercials, and other ancillary sources on the ground that actors' reputations are gained from performance in playwrights' plays.

This contest illustrates the running debate about what justifies ownership: Should it be production-of, contribution-to, need, merit, capture? But, however else it is justified, property serves an important survival function for groups, one that is implicit in a third attribute of its definition.

3. The notion of property *excludes.* It prohibits common use of something valued.

The exclusivity inherent in the notion of property is one of the two known ways of averting "the tragedy of the commons" (Hardin 1968a). The tragedy of the commons is that any *valued* resource— and that means any *limited* resource—will be depleted if everyone has access to it without limit. This is true of fish in the lakes, minerals in the ground, and silence in the mountains. Thus far, Man has invented only two procedures for averting this tragedy. One is to *assign rations* of the valued thing or activity by force. This is usually done by governments. The other procedure grants *property rights* in the valued resource. These rights refer to the power, backed by custom and state-enforced law, to use *exclusively* something of value.

This point brings to the fore one of the most heated controversies in political economics: that of the relative efficiency and utility of allocating use of scarce resources by government-imposed rationing or by a market in which privately owned goods can be exchanged. It is this controversy that underlies continuing debates about definitions of cheating and stealing.

Culture-binding

These comments on the meaning of property are intended to show that the ideas of wrong that suffuse notions of crime are contested. It is not our task to resolve these contests, but it will be clear that our discussion of "theft" in later chapters is culture-bound.

DISHONESTY

Two major modes by which we injure one another are by force and by fraud. We can, of course, combine the two processes as in some kinds of robbery where the victim is first "suckered" into a vulnerable position and then strong-armed. However, crimes that employ force seem more "honest" than those that employ fraud, depending on the dimension of honesty one has in mind.

To be honest, dictionaries tell us, is to be honorable, but it is also to be genuine, forthright, and truthful. Some homicides are deemed to be honorable, as we saw (Chapter 5, Volume Two), and they are, of course, genuine when they are intended. Similarly, armed robbery may or may not be dishonorable, depending on the side one takes,[3] but it is forthright. We have little doubt about what the robber is doing.

By contrast, the major modes by which we are dishonest are by lying, cheating, and thieving by fraud and stealth. Lying, cheating, fraud, and sneak-thieving depend on deception—on saying other than what one means, or being other than what one pretends to be, or concealing acts that harm others.

The deceptions that are called *lies* are those intended to convince others that some *act* is truthful when it is not. By "truthful," we mean true as a statement or probable as a promise. Lies, then, can be perpetrated by gesture or costume as well as by utterance. We "tell lies" with more than words.

---

[3] If one regards robbers as "social bandits" righting economic wrongs, such robbery is not dishonorable. Remember Robin Hood. Other examples of honorable robbery are provided by modern motion pictures. Many films justify robbery, not so much as achieving "social justice," but as an adventure justified by the glamour of the robbers. See "Fun and Games with Dick and Jane," "The Great Train Robbers," or "Rough Cut."

Moreover, we recognize a gradient of beneficent to harmful lies. There are polite lies, required lies, and damaging lies (Bok 1978, Ludwig 1965). Deceit is a major weapon in all contests for survival.

To cheat is intentionally to break a rule that is supposed to govern the relationship in which one is engaged. The violated rule can be that governing exchange of property, or that governing a social relationship such as that between spouses or between teacher and student, or it can be a rule of the game we've agreed to play.

To steal is, of course, illegally to appropriate another's property. Theft, by definition, becomes more "dishonest" as it is carried off by concealment or lying. (This does *not* mean that such theft becomes more criminal—that is, more heavily condemned or penalized). The wide range of larceny committed with the aid of lies is recognized as *fraud.*

In any larceny committed with deceit, there can be degrees of the mixture of concealment and outright lying. Embezzlement, for example, can be carried out as sneak thievery with varying amounts of lying, depending on the circumstances (Chapter 3).

Given these qualifications, it is useful to think of dishonesty as running along the three dimensions of lying, cheating, and concealed thieving. Any one deceitful episode—criminal or lawful—may employ mixtures of these dishonest procedures.[4]

Implications

These definitions have implications, some of which deserve comment.

To lie is to intend to deceive

People who believe the falsehoods they utter are not liars. True believers in false pictures of the world are something else—superstitious, incorrect, or "faith-full." They are not liars because to lie is to *intend* to mislead others.

Moreover, when a person intends to mislead others, the "lie" that she thinks she is saying may, in fact, be a true proposition (Mottershead 1980, p. 1). The heart of the lie is, again, in the intention to deceive rather than in the veridicality of the utterance. This point dis-

---

[4] This is said to remind us that only a limited amount of dishonesty is criminal.

tinguishes a lie from a mistake, and it says that a liar may tell a truth by accident.

These possibilities remind us that honestly held convictions may draw false maps of reality and may, then, be as damaging to their believers as some lies.

To tell a lie requires a conception of truth

An important implication of our definitions of dishonesty is that ability to recognize deceit—a lie or a cheat—rests on a conception of truth. Truth, in turn, rests on a conception of reality.

If reality becomes relativized, if it is only to be negotiated and never to be known, then drawing a distinction between a lie and a truth becomes difficult, if not impossible. Even with an agreed-upon conception of reality, a gray borderland persists between outright lies and clear truths. In this foggy area deceit lives by means of omission, deletion, and blurred concept.

Language is the principal instrument through which this zone of ambiguity is defended and enlarged. Words are the major weapons of the lie. This is an additional reason for keeping concepts clean. If language becomes corrupt, thought becomes misleading.[5]

This admonition applies most strongly in the political arena where fraud is a normal part of contest and where fraud fades away from blatant lying into slogan, cloudy statement, and truly believed nonsense.

Lying serves political functions

Everyone knows that etiquette involves privacy, reticence, inhibition. Challengers of a moral order call such politeness "lying." They are correct in that manners that lubricate social relations require the "deceit" of self-censorship. One does not do or say all that one is thinking.

But these polite lies are innocent compared with the consequences of lying for political purposes. Political intentions are those directed toward attaining and maintaining power. They constitute

---

[5] A professor of the humanities recently disturbed our dinner by urging criminologists to fight "academic terrorism" and "bureaucratic violence in the university." This advocate could not understand the difference between figurative and literal speech and that, by confusing the two, he was doing "violence" to language.

strong drives to deceive.[6] Seabury (1980) suggests that lying in the political forum serves three functions:

1. "To deceive your opponents about your intentions"

2. "To gull and win over the minds and hearts of the credulous to your cause. . . . To persuade, recruit, convince, and control. . . ."

3. "To assert [the state's] public uncontradictability and thus to confirm that those who rule cannot be publicly challenged. . . . The lie reminds everyone of its own impunity."

Definitions of dimensions of dishonesty, and their implications, provide a prelude to discussion in the following chapters of the varieties of deceitful crime. As prelude, three additional questions about dishonesty require attention:

1. Is honesty a personality trait?
2. If it is, who is more and less honest and when?
3. Can deceit be detected or predicted?

---

[6] In support of the thesis that the quest for power tends to corrupt language and therefore thought (fn. 5), Steigerwald (1980) notes politically inclined definitions in *Webster's New World Dictionary, 2nd College Edition* (1976). This is the "in-house" dictionary of the *New York Times,* Associated Press, United Press International, the *Washington Post, Los Angeles Times, The Wall Street Journal, Newsweek,* and more than 200 other news publications. Steigerwald comments:

Among *Webster's* . . . entries are brief identifications of some of the greatest tyrants of our age—Fidel Castro, Francisco Franco, Adolf Hitler, Ho Chi Minh, N. Lenin, Mao Tse-tung, Benito Mussolini, Joseph Stalin, and Tito. Yet not all despots are equally odious. According to *Webster's,* some tyrants are less tyrannical than others.

Only three of the nine rate the title of dictator, that is, "a ruler with absolute power and authority, esp. one who exercises it tyrannically."—[Hitler, Mussolini, and Franco].

Unlike these fascist dictators, the socialist despots in *Webster's* sound like a six-pack of Lions Club officers. Joe Stalin is Soviet Premier . . . Lenin is Russian leader [and] premier of the Soviet Union . . . Mao is Chinese communist leader, chairman of the People's Republic of China. Ho Chi Minh is president of North Vietnam. Castro and Tito are leaders, prime ministers, and presidents. . . . Ho Chi Minh and Richard Nixon are both described as presidents. . . . Yet the dictionary's own definition of Communism is "a hypothetical stage of socialism . . . to be achieved by revolutionary and dictatorial, rather than gradualistic, means." . . . Though the bias in *Webster's New World* is probably not deliberate . . . the fact that the myth of no-dictators-on-the-left thrives in an apolitical reference book so widely accepted and used is not encouraging. The totalitarian governments of socialist-Communist states have attained a legitimacy they don't deserve.

1. Generality of Honesty

We have held that the idea of "personality" is an idea of continuity (Chapter 3, Volume One). If there were no stability in individual conduct across situations and through time, there would be no "identity" to identify. People would not be *persons;* they would be units reacting to situations.

The idea that human beings are persons connotes some stability, but it does not require rigidity. However personality is conceived, it is recognized as a bundle of dispositions whose exercise in action varies with situations. All psychologists are *interactionists* of some sort. The interesting questions are *how much* of conduct persists in the "constitution" of the person as she ages and moves from here to there and *how much* of conduct can be expected to change with these moves.

Psychologists Hartshorne and May and their associates (1928–1930) attempted to answer these questions as they concern honest action. They gave American schoolchildren a variety of opportunities to lie, cheat, and steal. Children had a chance to cheat on tests of reading, spelling, arithmetic, information, and grammar; in solving puzzles and in parlor games. The investigators also invented ways of tempting children to steal coins without being observed, but in a manner that allowed the theft to be recorded. And they gave children opportunities to make false statements on questionnaires where there were two kinds of motive for lying: to win approval and to escape disapproval. Technically, these measures of false statement were not tests of "lying" since the psychologists could not distinguish intent to deceive from mistake.

The three dimensions of deceit run together, but with varying degrees of closeness. For example, there is a closer relationship between one kind of cheating and another, and between lying and cheating, than there is between cheating or lying and stealing. The more similar the style of deceit, obviously, the greater the consistency of conduct.

Hartshorne and May interpreted their results as showing positive associations across dimensions of honesty, but they believed the correlations were too low to allow one to speak of a general trait of honesty. However, Burton (1963) recalculated the original data, omitting from his analysis those tests that were unreliable. Among the reliable measures of behavior, Burton found a *general tendency* for children to be more or less honest. "There is," he concludes, "an underlying trait of honesty which a person brings with him to a resistance to temptation situation" (p. 492).

More recent studies of resistance to temptation reach a similar conclusion. Individuals behave rather consistently in a variety of situations that tempt them to lie or cheat and these dimensions of deceit correlate to a lesser degree with vulnerability to stealing. Situations make a difference in rule-breaking, of course, but persons make more of a difference than situations. That is, individuals produce more of the variability in conduct than do situations (Barbu 1951, Furman & Masters 1980, Kipnis 1968, Nelsen et al. 1969, Schaie & Parham 1976). Dramatically changed circumstances can shift the standard of conduct in one direction or another, and can constrict or expand the range of possibilities, but individual differences persist in such a way as to make it reasonable to speak of character and of traits.

We come to the same conclusion if, instead of testing for dishonesty, we test for the converse: "pro-social" behaviors such as caring, sharing, and helping. Mussen and Eisenberg-Berg (1977) summarize longitudinal research employing a variety of measures of altruistic action. Positive correlations appear between dimensions of altruism, justifying its conception as a trait. Furthermore, this trait characterizes persons as they mature, but more consistently for boys than for girls. Mussen and Eisenberg-Berg write:

> Impressive evidence of cross-situation consistency (generality) and the stability of prosocial behavior comes from a longitudinal study that began with extensive and intensive observations of nursery school boys and girls. During the first observational period, nurturance and sympathy to other children, thoughtfulness, and understanding the viewpoints of peers were all related in ways that suggested an underlying predisposition to social responsibility and altruism. The same boys and girls were systematically observed again in elementary school five or six years later. Again at this time, socially responsible and altruistic behaviors were associated with each other. Most striking from the point of view of across-time consistency or stability were the correlations between behavior indicative of social responsibility and altruism during the nursery school period and comparable behavior (independently observed) five or six years later ($r = .60$ for boys and $.36$ for girls) (p. 22).

Since people can be ranked along a continuum of honest action, varying somewhat with circumstance, the next questions ask who behaves more and less honestly and when.

2. Differential Distribution of Dishonesty

Honest action is probably distributed in large populations in the same fashion as is foolish action. To rephrase Lincoln, some people are honest all the time, some are honest none of the time, and most people are honest some of the time.

Tallies of conduct are limited, of course. They are limited as regards kinds of behavior observed and as regards spans of time and populations surveyed. Given this qualification, most people seem to be "middling honest." The meaning of this phrase is given by one of the best-controlled tallies of honesty—Hartshorne and May's *cheating ratio.* Their studies of deceit included ten tests on which children could cheat. The investigators computed a ratio between the number of cheats and the number of chances to cheat:

$$\text{Cheating ratio} = \frac{\text{Number of cheats}}{\text{Number of chances to cheat}}$$

A ratio of 1.00 means that people with such a score cheat every chance they get. A ratio of 0.00 means that people with such a score never cheat despite the opportunity to do so. Table 1.1 shows the distribution of cheating ratios among 2,443 school children. The table says that 3.2 percent cheated all the time while 7.0 percent cheated none of the time. About half the children cheated on between one-third and two-thirds of the chances they had and about 13 percent cheated half the time.

Table 1.1   Distribution of Cheating Ratios Among School Children*

Cheating ratio	Number	Percent**
1.00	78	3.2
.90	105	4.3
.80	178	7.3
.70	231	9.4
.60	252	10.3
.50	308	12.6
.40	310	12.7
.30	439	17.9
.20	231	9.4
.10	140	5.7
.00	171	7.0

*Reprinted, with permission, from Hartshorne and May, *Studies in the Nature of Character.* Vol. 1, p. 379. © 1928–1930 by Macmillan Book Company.

**Percentages do not add to 100 because of rounding.

These numbers parallel less rigorous measures of honesty in juvenile and adult populations. A shortcoming of most studies of character is the lack of a ratio between acts and opportunities. Allowing for this, deceitful crime seems to approximate a normal distribution with few doing much, few doing little, and most doing some such crime. The distributions vary, of course, with gravity of the offense. A sample of such distributions illustrates the point.

Table 1.2   Percentage of Boys Who Have Ever Committed Certain Thefts, Graded by Level of Seriousness*

Type of Theft	Percentage Admitting to It			
	Level 1	Level 2	Level 3	Level 4
Stealing from a shop	70	53	37	16
Cheating someone out of money	68	47	27	7
Stealing money	58	51	39	22
Stealing from someone at school	49	35	27	8
"Pinching" things from family or relations	47	35	21	8
Stealing something out of a garden or yard	37	31	22	10
Stealing from a cafe	34	21	10	2
Stealing from work	32	25	18	8
Stealing from a building site	31	27	21	11
Stealing from a car, lorry, or van	25	23	19	13
Stealing by breaking and entering	18	17	15	11
Stealing from a changing-room or cloakroom	18	15	12	5

*Adapted, with permission, from W. A. Belson et al. *Juvenile Theft: The Causal Factors.* Table 2.1 © 1975 by William A. Belson. Published by Harper & Row, Ltd.

Belson and Associates' Study

Belson and his colleagues (1975) used a reliable form of interviewing to elicit English boys' admissions of theft. Almost 1,500 London boys, 13 to 16 years of age, responded anonymously to questions about 44 kinds of stealing, most of it sneak-thievery. Table 1.2

shows the proportions of boys who confessed to the more interesting of these crimes. This table categorizes thefts by value of the
objects stolen. Level 1 includes things worth less than 1 shilling, 6
pence in 1970 British funds. Level 2 ranges from that lower limit to
things worth less than 4/6d; level 3 from 4/6d to things worth less
than £1; and level 4 ranges from that lower limit and higher.

Depending on one's expectations, Table 1.2 can be interpreted to
say that stealing is not uncommon and that the popularity of theft declines as the value of the theft increases.

Belson and his co-workers also counted the varieties of thievery
admitted by their subjects. These findings can be summarized as indicating that about one-fourth of the boys have committed more
than half of the 44 kinds of theft at least once and the average boy has
committed 18 of these crimes.

Other Controlled Observations

Other studies, smaller in scale, tell us something about the distribution of deceitful crimes.

Riis (1941a, b, c) reports a series of tests conducted for *The
Reader's Digest* toward the end of America's business depression.
Men and women, appearing as couples, toured garages and radio and
watch repair shops. The automobiles, radios, and watches that they
submitted for repairs had been deliberately "jimmied" to make them
seem to be out of order. The test of honesty was a tally of the number of shops that made charges for false repairs. Riis reports that:

> Of 347 garages visited, 63 percent were dishonest.
> Of 304 radio repair shops visited, 64 percent were dishonest.
> Of 462 watch repair shops visited, 49 percent were dishonest.

Critics of *The Reader's Digest* survey have suggested that much of
the fraud uncovered was caused by the poor business climate of the
Depression years. This might explain Riis's findings without erasing
them. Another explanation of these terrible figures is that what appeared to be fraud may have been incompetence.

The possibility that incompetence may be mistaken for fraud is a
real one. However, the suggestion that it was "only the Depression"
that moved repairmen to cheat their customers is challenged by a recent study of garage work in New York City. *The New York Times*
tested the honesty of automobile repair shops in a manner similar to
that used by the *Digest's* study. Thirteen out of 24 garages visited
either wrongly diagnosed the test car's "defect," lending substance to

the idea of incompetence, or recommended expensive and unnecessary repairs (Bacon 1976).

Feldman (1968) and his co-workers tested the relative honesty of French, Greek, and American adults in a variety of situations that gave people opportunities to cheat fellow citizens and foreigners. For example, investigators asked strangers for directions in Paris, Athens, and Boston. They did this in fluent French, Greek, and Boston-accented English, but they also conducted their tests as foreigners who could not speak the language of the country. The researchers also overpaid cashiers in stores and observed who kept the overcharge, and they counted tendencies of taxi drivers to cheat native and foreign customers. Another test noted which individuals made false claims for money from a stranger.

As travel experience and stereotype suggest, Parisian taxi drivers cheated American tourists significantly more frequently than they did their fellow Frenchmen, and they did so in an ingenious number of ways. Similarly, cashiers who were overpaid "kept the change" in 54 percent of the Parisian stores, 51 percent of the Athenian shops, and 33 percent of the Boston stores. On the other hand, false claims for money were made by only 6 percent of Parisians, as compared with 13 percent of Athenians and 17 percent of the Bostonians sampled.

Merritt and Fowler (1948) conducted a test of another style of honesty. Their assistants casually dropped stamped, addressed postcards and envelopes on streets of American cities. Some of the envelopes contained a lead coin that felt like a 50-cent piece. Their tally of temptation was the differential in posting of these three kinds of valuable. They found that 72 percent of the postcards were mailed and 85 percent of the envelopes containing letters. But of the letters with fake coins inside, only 54 percent were posted.

Conclusion

Such tests of public honesty could be extended. They confirm the popularity of predation by deceit, at least in more open societies. They lend substance to the cynical journalist's definition of honesty as "deficiency of reach" (Bierce 1958). They second the judgment of the Scottish philosopher David Hume (1711–1776) that "A man who at noon leaves his purse full of gold on the pavement at Charing Cross may as well expect that it will fly away like a feather as that he will find it untouched an hour after" (1955, p. 100).

Bierce and Hume were correct, for San Francisco and London, then and now. But they are less correct if the scene is shifted to

Riyadh, Saudi Arabia, 1980. This tells us something about the contingencies affecting theft. Research adds to our picture of who is more and less vulnerable to the temptation to deceive.

Contingencies

Some of the contingencies affecting displays of dishonesty can be outlined without elaboration of the research leading to these conclusions.

1. Spreading the pain stimulates larceny. The more distant, diffuse, and anonymous the victim of theft, the more people who will steal from it (Smigel & Ross 1970). Theft from universities, corporations, and governments seems less dishonest to most people than theft from an individual.

2. Big theft, and rare theft, carried off with flair, seems less dishonest than ordinary stealing and undramatic larceny. A small-town banker cheated his customers of an estimated $5 million in one of the largest solo embezzlements in United States history. Yet many of his acquaintances felt, "Well, he got caught and should be punished, but he is still a good old guy" (Maxwell 1972, 1973).

In a similar vein, the first American skyjacker to parachute with an extorted fortune became a folk hero with his name printed on T-shirts and copy-cats trying to duplicate his feat.

3. People who have experienced failure are more likely to cheat (Fry 1975, 1976). This finding conforms with the repeated observation that juvenile delinquents do poorly in school (Kelly & Pink 1973, Phillips & Kelly 1979).

4. People who are disliked and who dislike themselves tend to be more deceitful (Aronson & Mettee 1968, Furman & Masters 1980, Kaplan 1976, Mussen et al. 1970).

5. People who are impulsive, distractable, and unable to postpone gratification are more likely to engage in deceitful crime (Barndt & Johnson 1955, Davids & Falkof 1975, Grim et al. 1968, Kipnis 1968, Offer et al. 1979, Roberts et al. 1974, Stein et al. 1968).

6. People "with a conscience" are more resistant to temptation to deceive (Belson et al. 1975, Rettig & Pasamanick 1964). Conscience here refers to the *importance* an individual attaches to being caught and censured.

7. Honest people are more consistently honest than dishonest people are consistently dishonest (Hartshorne & May 1928–1930).

8. Intelligent people tend to be more honest than stupid people

(Burton 1963, Hartshorne & May 1928–1930). The correlation is modest, but significant.

This finding from non-reactive research methods[7] corroborates the long-noted *negative* relationship between officially recorded juvenile delinquency and IQ (Austin 1978, Ganzer & Sarason 1973). American criminologists have tended to doubt this correlation. Hirschi and Hindelang (1977, 1978) review the history of denial of this association and show that "IQ has an effect on delinquency independent of class and race, and . . . this effect is mediated through a host of school variables" (1977, p. 571).

Among adult official offenders, intelligence varies considerably with the kind of criminal work performed, just as it does among legitimate jobs (Tulchin 1971).

9. The connection between *knowing* "what is right" and *doing* right is loose. Research yields conflicting results on the relationship between verbal tests of moral judgment and good conduct (Blasi 1980).

On the one hand, some studies report that youths who score *low* on tests of moral judgment are also more likely to cheat and steal (Krebs 1968, Schwartz et al. 1969). On the other hand, the Hartshorne and May tests found no relationship or a negative relationship between "mouth morality" and morality in deed. Burton (1963, p. 498) notes:

> Boys tend to be more honest and more consistent on the Hartshorne and May temptation tests, but girls tend to appear more conforming to the general moral code as measured by verbal tests or ratings by parents and teachers.

Another observer (Lickona 1976, p. 202) puts the point this way:

> The gap between moral reasoning and behavior may yawn wide even in history's moral heroes. Gore Vidal's *Burr* levels this charge against Thomas Jefferson: "Proclaiming the unalienable rights of man for everyone (except slaves, Indians, women and those entirely without property), Jefferson tried to seize the Floridas by force, dreamed of a conquest of

---

[7] A "non-reactive method" is one that is relatively immune to instrument error, that is, to having the behavior measured contaminated by the mode of measurement. For example, police records of criminal activity are accused of being reactive measures, biased by factors other than the conduct of those apprehended. This accusation is more and less valid depending on the police department and the kind of crime being counted. One is more confident of any tally of events as one method produces results similar to other procedures.

> Cuba, and after his illegal purchase of Louisiana sent a military governor to rule New Orleans against the will of its inhabitants. . . . It was of course Jefferson's gift at one time or another to put with eloquence the 'right' answer to every moral question. In practice, however, he seldom deviated from an opportunistic course, calculated to bring him power."

It seems advisable, again, not to confuse what people say with what they do.

10. Middle- and upper-class people tend to be more honest than lower-class people (Feldman 1968, Hartshorne & May 1928–1930). This statement applies to those segments of deceitful action that have been observed unobtrusively in controlled tests. No one has calculated lying, cheating, and stealing ratios in all their variety, and we assume that social class differences are a matter of thresholds rather than a matter of absolutes.

Age makes a difference here; the correlations between socio-economic status and tests of deceitful behavior increase as youngsters move from childhood into adolescence. Moreover, the higher the status, the more consistent is the honest behavior (Burton 1963).

These correlations from unobtrusive observations confirm data from official records of criminal behavior. Official records have deficiencies, of course, and critical sociologists have argued that their association with categories of social class reflects police bias more than it does class-linked differences in conduct. Such few non-reactive studies as are available refute the charge that it is only judicial bias, and not differences in behavior, that accounts for arrest patterns.

11. The easier it is to cheat and steal, the more people who will do so (Hall 1890, Hartshorne & May 1928–1930). This is hardly news except for those who have assumed that there is *no* threshold of temptation for people who are vaguely defined as "really honest." To the contrary, as gangsters assure us, "Everyone has a price."

Unobtrusive observations record this fact of life, a fact that should *not* be interpreted as saying that the *value* of any deceitful gain is equal for all people. Individuals have different "needs" and therefore different levels at which they will be moved to lie, cheat, or steal. However, Cohen and Felson (1979) show that one important concatenation of events that affects the amount of theft is "the convergence in space and time of *likely offenders, suitable targets,* and the *absence of capable guardians* against crime" (p. 588, emphasis in the original).

In brief, the more things available for theft, and the lower the probability of penalty, the more larceny.

12. Lying, cheating, and stealing increase as people strive for im-

portant objectives, with great pressure on them to achieve, and with limited ability or opportunity to attain their goals (Hall 1890, Pearline et al. 1967). The struggle to survive generates deceit.

This is probably the most well-traveled road to fraud. It is, for example, the route followed by American universities that "need" to have winning teams in lucrative sports like football and basketball (Papanek 1979, Reid 1979, Underwood 1980). It is also the path taken by the Soviet Union as it claims that success in sport demonstrates the superiority of "socialist man." This "demonstration" produces cheating in team competition at chess and in the Olympic Games of 1976 and 1980 (ABC 1980, Moore 1980, *Wall Street Journal* 1980c).

This is the same course by which major American cities have moved toward bankruptcy with the aid of "creative accounting" that "cooks the books" and conceals a city's true financial status. During the 1970s, Boston, Chicago, Cleveland, New York City, and other metropolitan areas faced financial disaster, and their troubles continue (Adams 1979, 1980, Auletta 1975a, 1975b, Greene 1980). An auditing firm's study of the practices in America's 50 largest cities found "shoddy and misleading accounting" to be widespread (Greene 1980).

Incompetence may explain part of these fiscal follies, but a stronger cause is the political urge to promise, and to give, and to pass the costs of one's acts to distant others and future generations.

Similar pressure to deceive occurs in communist lands where production quotas imposed upon farmers and factory managers cause them to fake their accounts. This road to fraud appears in states as diverse as The People's Republic of China, Cuba, Hungary, and the Soviet Union (Berliner 1961, Bethel 1980b, Calzon 1978, Chalidze 1977, Ching 1980, Cohen 1968, 1977, Cooney 1979, Hooper 1980, Leng 1977, Marton 1979).

Legal work in commerce, in politics, and in warfare generates deceit. Competition makes deceit a rational tactic. For example, "game theorists" who teach courses in business negotiation can demonstrate that "hiding certain facts, bluffing, or even outright lying often gets . . . a better deal" (Bulkeley 1979, p. 1). In his course in "Competitive Decision Making" at Harvard, Howard Raiffa refers to such practices as "strategic misrepresentation." Raiffa contends that such maneuvering is important, not because it teaches students to lie, but because it makes them aware that in bargaining they are apt to be lied to. This is a lesson that an American president learned late in life, at cost to his constituents, when he complained, December, 1979, that he was shocked to find that Communist leaders had lied to him.

However immoral it may be regarded, lying can be a rational strategy. It can be particularly rational when one's individual desires are to be achieved through some public process in which individual votes are aggregated to make a "social decision." In such circumstances, the economist Arrow (1978) proves that:

> Once a machine for making social choices from individual tastes is established, individuals will find it profitable, from a rational point of view, to misrepresent their tastes by their actions, either because such misrepresentation is somehow directly profitable or, more usually, because some other individual will be made so much better off by the first individual in such a way that both are better off than if everyone really acted in direct accordance with his tastes (p. 7).

In summary, all competitive situations make deceit a sometimes rational means to one's end. Thresholds of resistance to this temptation vary with individual and cultures, of course. Latin cultures, for example, regard more lying and cheating as normal than do Nordic cultures (Gaither 1961).

Deceit is best contained by the kind of training that a moral community can provide. This requires discipline in obeying rules of the game, and discipline requires practice. Since open, heterogeneous societies are *not* "moral communities," deceit is to be expected in the public arena.

Knowledge of the contingencies through which people are differentially motivated to lie, cheat, and steal can be used as generally self-protective information. However, this information is not sufficiently fine to permit predictive statements for groups or individuals about the *level* at which any of these conditions produces *a certain quantity* of deceit. Nevertheless, we are constantly engaged in evaluating other's promises and performances, and the ability to detect deception has survival value. The fact that so many people lie to us so often makes detection of deception one of our most important daily forms of "relating" to others. This raises questions about how well we can detect deceit and by what signs.

3. Detecting Deceit

All attempts to detect deceit rely on one or two assumptions and their combination: that telling a lie carries a cost and that more dishonest persons wear signs of their difference from more honorable people.

The cost of deception is believed to be readable in involuntary physiological responses. The signs of a cheating character are believed to be legible in mannerism and costume. Folk sayings give advice of this nature:

"She looks you in the eye" = She is honest.
"He offers you a wet hand" = He's a crook.
"He wears his hat askew" = Watch out!

There *are* indicators of deceit, but their accuracy is limited. Their limitation means that, as with other psychological tests, we pay a price in a proportion of false positive bets for the sake of a proportion of true positive hits (Lykken 1979, 1981).

Procedures

Human beings have tried to detect deceit since the beginning of history. Magic and torture have been the principal means used to distinguish liars from truth-tellers. Both continue to be employed. Modern tyrants regularly use torture, and even "civilized" societies use pain and its threat to extract the truth.

More ethical procedures, by our standards, include use of hypnosis or sedatives to "reduce resistance." We also attend to emotional behavior as a sign of deception.

Hypnosis and depressant agents are sometimes useful in recovering memories from confused patients (Hilgard 1977, Wolberg 1948), but their utility as "truth-pullers" from willful liars has not been demonstrated. Sodium amytal, sodium pentothal, and scopolamine have all been recommended as alleged "truth serums." They are supposed to reduce inhibition and thus allow investigators to extract confessions from otherwise reluctant suspects. However, experiments have demonstrated that subjects can continue to lie even under narcosis (Morland 1958, p. 148).

Detection of deception from signs of emotion is more promising. The assumption underlying these tests is that, for most people, the act of deceiving others produces involuntary physiological changes that can be discerned. On an informal basis all people whose work involves assessing the veracity of others employ such signs. The Chinese, for example, have used the pupillary reflex as a sign of emotionality—a dilated pupil allegedly indicating attention and, possibly, the physiological cost of deceit (Hess 1965). Another Oriental test gives the suspect a mouthful of rice and requires him or her to spit it out. The supposition is that a guilty conscience makes it difficult to salivate. The dry mouth that cannot spit is allegedly a sign of deceit.

Salespeople, detectives, and others concerned with detecting deceit use additional folk rules. For example, they observe voice tremors and "parapraxes"—slips of the tongue, delayed speech, stuttering, umms, and ughs. They watch for excessive movement—fidgets, leg-rubbing, hand-wringing, finger-clenching. Perspiring is a sensitive indicator of emotion and, hence, possibly of lying. Wet palms and beads of sweat on the upper lip reveal strain.

The face is a "fast-sending system" of nonverbal communication. It is equipped to express emotion and it may, therefore, "leak" information against the sender's wishes (Ekman & Friesen 1969, 1975). Eye contact has long been thought to be a valid indicator of honesty and deviation from some norm of gaze interaction has been thought to signal deception. However, all con-artists know this folk belief and they discipline themselves to "look you in the eye" as they defraud you. There is evidence that involuntary twitches of the mouth—suppressed grinning, for example—may more accurately reveal the liar than eye movement or averted gaze (Dunlap 1927, Howells 1938).

These, and other, folk indicators will continue to be used because human relations require constant interpretation of others as truth-sayers or deceivers. However, when tallies are made of the accuracy of such popular procedures, their detection record is poor (Podlesny & Raskin 1978, Raskin et al. 1976). The situation here is similar to that in job interviews. Interviewers who have *confidence* in their ability to judge others and to foretell others' probable success in a job have poor records as predictors of performance (Blenkner 1954, Bloom & Brundage 1947, Dunlap & Wantman 1944, Einhorn & Hogarth 1978, Kelly & Fiske 1950, Wiggins & Kohen 1971).

The poor record of popular readings of deceit has led to a search for scientific tests of honesty. Scientific tests differ from common procedures for knowing others in that they attempt to reduce the "human variable." That is, they aspire to be objective in the sense that their results do not depend on the varying inclinations of individual judges. An objective test is one that gives reliable readings by numbers of trained administrators of the test.

The lie detection industry now finds employment in espionage, in personnel selection, and in criminalistics. Lykken (1974) reports that:

> Several *million* polygraphic examinations are conducted annually [in the United States] by more than 3,000 professional polygraphers, most of whom are engaged in the private practice of their art, and some dozen schools, including one operated by the U.S. Army, are spawning graduates (p. 725, emphasis his).

A first fact to be recognized about this work is that *none* of the devices used are lie detectors. They are emotion detectors. Deceit is *inferred* from changes in some indicators of emotion as stimuli move from the innocuous to the significant. Everything rests, then, on the differentiating power of emotional signs *and* on the inferences drawn from those signs. Detecting deception requires knowing *what* to count as its indicator and *how* to draw a conclusion from the tallies.

Polygraph and Voice Strain Evaluations

Professional lie detectors have worked with two devices in five ways. The most popular instrument is the *polygraph* which, as its name suggests, takes simultaneous, multiple readings of emotional indicators. The usual instrument measures perspiration via changes in palmar skin resistance to passage of an electric current (the galvanic skin response or GSR). At the same time, an arm plethysmograph records changes in size of the upper arm as an indicator of heart rate and blood volume. And, simultaneously, expansible belts around the subject's chest and abdomen record thoracic and abdominal respiration rates.

Questions relevant and irrelevant to the crime are then asked and emotional responses are noted. The mode of interrogation has taken three forms.

The Truth Control Test (TCT)

In the truth control test, responses to questions concerning the crime under investigation are compared with responses to questions about a fake crime. It is assumed that a stronger physiological response will be given by a guilty person to relevant questions about the actual crime than to control questions about a nonexistent crime. It is also assumed that an innocent person will respond more or less equally to both questions. This test is seldom used by professional lie detectors.

The Lie Control Test (LCT)

The lie control test is the standard form of polygraph interrogation. The suspect is run through a set of questions including relevant, irrelevant, and control items. A sample set devised to test truthfulness in a rape case appears in Table 1.3.

It is assumed that a guilty person will be more strained by the relevant questions than by the control questions, even if (s)he lies on the control questions too. Conversely, it is assumed that an innocent person will be less strained by the relevant questions. If the suspect responds more strongly to the control questions, (s)he is called "truthful."

Table 1.3   A Typical Lie Control Test*

1. Is today Tuesday?	(Irrelevant)
2. Are you concerned that I might ask you a question that we have not reviewed?	(Outside Issue)
3. Regarding the incident with Mary V., do you intend to tell me the truth about that?	(Sacrifice Relevant)
4. On the night of May 15th, did you force your way into Mary V.'s motel room?	(Relevant)
5. Have you ever committed an abnormal sex act?	(Control)
6. On the night of May 15th, did you threaten to choke Mary V.?	(Relevant)
7. Prior to last year, have you ever forced a woman to have sex with you?	(Control)
8. Is your name Sam?	(Irrelevant)
9. Prior to last year, did you ever lie to someone in authority to get out of trouble?	(Control)
10. On the night of May 15th, did you rape Mary V.?	(Relevant)

*Reproduced, with permission, from D.T. Lykken, "Polygraphic interrogation: The applied psychophysiologist." In A. Gale and J. Edwards (eds.), *Physiological Correlates of Human Behavior.* © 1980 by Academic Press.

The Guilty Knowledge Test (GKT)

The guilty knowledge test assumes that a guilty person will know some facts about a case that an innocent suspect cannot know. It is assumed, then, that a guilty person will show stronger emotional response to a "significant" stimulus than will an innocent person who is ignorant of the relevance of the cue to the crime. The responses of suspects are gauged according to the differential effect produced by words, or other symbols, associated with the crime as compared with control words or images. The test, again, is a measure of *difference* in emotionality signaled by the suspect as cue symbols and control symbols are presented.

The guilty knowledge test can be administered as a series of multiple-choice questions or as questions or pictures presented to the subject *without* requiring the subject to say anything. Emotion can be recorded without the suspect's doing more than looking or listening. Furthermore, the guilty knowledge test can be applied:

> Whether [the suspect] is high or low in reactivity, whether he has confidence in the test or not, whether he is frightened and aroused or calm and indifferent . . . [Under all these conditions] we can still expect that his response to this significant alternative will be stronger than to the other alternatives as long as he recognizes which alternative is "correct" (Lykken 1974, p. 728).

The guilty knowledge test has additional advantages in that it can produce "an objective, quantitative estimate of the probability of guilt, and . . . in certain situations . . . is capable of yielding near-perfect validity" (Lykken 1974, p. 729). This test is particularly useful as an instrument with which to clear innocent suspects. Used in this way, it is an aid to police efficiency. However, the guilty knowledge test cannot be used in most of the situations in which the polygraph is now used: To screen employees and to ascertain probable guilt or innocence where information is lacking with which to construct such an examination.

Voice Strain Assessment

A second device employed in emotion detection records changes in voice pattern as questions relevant and irrelevant to the crime are asked. Chapter 3, Volume One, mentioned voice as a personality constant and the use of voiceprints to identify individuals. Here an attempt is made to record emotional changes from changes in speech. Graphic representations of tonal qualities ("spectrograms" or "spectrographs") are used in two ways to detect deception. One method inspects the range of sound frequencies and looks for changes as "loaded" questions are asked. A second procedure, the *Psychological Stress Evaluator (PSE)*, attends to the proportion of *low* frequencies in speech on the assumption that these tend to *decrease* under psychological tension. An advantage of PSE for investigators is that it can be used without a subject's compliance or knowledge.

Validity

None of these procedures is foolproof. The *Guilty Knowledge Test* has the greatest possibility of *clearing innocent suspects*. Thus far, it also has a respectable record in detecting guilt. In laboratory studies, Lykken (1980, pp. 24–25) reports 100 percent accuracy in identifying the innocent and 80 to 95 percent accuracy in identifying the guilty.

But this record has not been tested with actual criminal cases. We noted limitations of this test earlier.

Polygraph testing via the *Lie Control Test* has a fair to good record in detecting guilty persons, but it does so at the cost of wrongly classifying many innocent persons. The LCT is subject to error because of the possible intrusion of factors irrelevant to the guilt or innocence of the subject. These factors include the differential emotionality of individuals, their differences in fear of the consequences of the test, their confidence in the accuracy of the test, and examiners' subjective assessments of the suspect. In addition, examiners do not read polygraph cues in the most efficient manner.

Examiners *interpret* polygraph recordings, and their reading of the signs of deceit is intuitive rather than objective. For example, Szucko and Kleinmuntz (1981) conducted an experiment in which they assigned 15 psychology undergraduates to a "campus foray" that tempted them to steal while 15 other students were assigned to an innocent campus stroll. Six experienced polygraph interpreters then attempted to distinguish the thieves from the innocent, with the advantage of knowing that half of their sample had stolen something.

This experiment demonstrates, once again, that actuaries are better predictors than insightful interpreters. Szucko and Kleinmuntz note that "a simple linear combination of the cues outperformed all the judges without exception" (p. 492).

A statistical formula beats judges because human interpreters have limited memories, do not use information optimally, and apply decision rules inconsistently. And again, such accuracy as judges possess when they read polygraph records is purchased at the cost of false positive errors. Furthermore, neither experience nor training is associated with judges' accuracy, and attempts to improve intuitive judgment through training have not been promising (Goldberg & Rorer 1965, Hammond et al. 1973). *If* the "lie detector" is to be used at all— and its use is increasingly under challenge—then a discriminating equation should be substituted for fallible human interpretation.

Field Tests

Tests of the validity of the LCT and the *Psychological Stress Evaluator* in the field, as opposed to the laboratory, are difficult to conduct for many reasons, paramount among them being the difficulty of ascertaining who really is guilty or innocent. To date, there have been no field tests of the validity of the PSE. Two field studies of the LCT have been conducted well enough to permit conclusions about the validity of this method.

Horvath (1977) had ten professional polygraphers interpret readings from 56 criminal suspects. Half of these suspects later confessed and are known to have lied on the test. Half were later cleared of suspicion by the confession of another person. Horvath's examiners scored 63 percent of the 56 protocols as "deceptive." They accurately identified 77 percent of the guilty suspects, but at the price of incorrectly identifying 49 percent of the innocent.

Barland & Raskin (1976) report findings from tests of 109 suspects. Barland conducted the examinations with Raskin reading the protocols blindly.[8] If we *omit* those cases in which guilt or innocence could not be established and those that Raskin scored as "inconclusive," then this examination correctly classified 98 percent of the guilty suspects at the cost of incorrectly classifying 55 percent of the innocent.

These two field tests agree closely. Lykken (1980, p. 27) concludes his assessment of the LCT by saying that "validity ranges from 63 to 72% (where 50% equals chance expectancy) and about 50% of truthful respondents are erroneously classified as deceptive."

"Beating" the LCT

John Reid, inventor of the LCT, suggested that one could "beat" the lie detector by *raising* one's physiological responses to the *control* questions in ways that the examiner could not detect. This can be done, for example, by pressing one's arm on the chair, biting one's tongue, contracting the toes, tightening buttocks, or secreting a tack in one's sock and pressing on it at the appropriate time.

Lykken (1980, pp. 21–22) reports that an inmate who was doing a long term for murder after having failed the LCT tested these procedures for "beating" the test with fellow convicts. In his prison all inmates accused of prison violations (smuggling drugs, fermenting booze, making weapons) are required to submit to an LCT. The convict "psychologist" advised 16 of his colleagues, all of whom admitted their guilt to him, how to fake their responses. All the men who followed his instructions "beat" the test.

Advice

Studies of the validity of LCT scores and of the possibility of faking them suggest this caution: *If you are innocent, don't take the test.*

---

[8] "Blind interpretation" means that evaluators do not know the identities of the cases they are judging nor do they know which are guilty and which innocent.

Uses

Given the probable prices of lie detection tests, experts disagree about their proper uses. For example, in Great Britain no "outside interference with the free will of the questioned persons is permitted" in criminal investigation (Morland 1960, p. 148). In similar vein, Minnesota law prohibits employers "from requiring or even requesting any employee or prospective employee to take a polygraph examination" (Lykken 1974, p. 738).

In Canada and the United States today, the polygraph is used principally as an instrument with which to extract confessions. However, Tarlow (1975) concludes an evaluation of American use of polygraph charts in jury trials by noting that juries are skeptical of the accuracy of such evidence and correctly use polygraph interpretations as an *aid* in judging the truthfulness of witnesses. Given the popularity of perjury, juries need all the help they can get.

Special Categories of Deceiver

Discussion of the difficulties in telling who is lying requires notice of three special categories of deceiver: Pathological liars, psychopathic liars, and self-deceivers.

Pathological Liars

Pathological lying is a relatively rare phenomenon, although the behavior bears resemblance to the more common practice of deceiving oneself. We reserve the title of pathological liar for those few people who seem unable to sense the difference between their telling a lie and their telling the truth, and who habitually lie. That is, these people prefer lying to speaking truly even when there seems to be "no good reason" for them to lie. We often say of such people, "They believe their own lies." Their lying runs a gamut, of course, from exaggerating the truth to inventing wild stories.

As we get to know such individuals, we discern two motives for their persistent deception. One is not to be trapped; the other is to appear glamorous.

The first motive, a facet of paranoia, is the feeling that inquisitors mean one no good and that it is always better, as personal policy, to throw out false cues than to reveal one's self.

This motive generates "pathological lying" only when the actors seem *unable* to discriminate deception from honesty. This qualification is required because lying for this paranoid reason is common in "societies" based on distrust. For example, Latin cultures in the

Mediterranean and the Americas assume that most people outside one's family intend no beneficence (Banfield 1958). People in such cultures assume the constancy of ill will and they believe that others' maleficent wishes have effects. Consequently, one divulges no plans and conceals any success. The "evil eye" is a metaphor for envy, and false signals are a defense against it.

Psychopathic Liars

Psychopathic liars differ from pathological liars, if only by degree, in that they are less confused about the difference between truth and falsehood. Psychopaths know that they are lying, and they enjoy telling lies. Everyone enjoys some "harmless fooling" of others, but psychopaths take pleasure in "jiving and conning." Their pleasure is instrumental—it is used to take advantage—but it is also expressive—it is an end in itself.

Both pathological and psychopathic liars give lie detectors difficulties. They do not respond as strongly, physiologically, to the pangs of conscience as do normal persons. They have little conscience to be pained. Truth does not have much salience. Therefore, lying is not important either. If the difference between telling the truth and telling a lie is blurred, and if, in addition, telling the truth is unimportant and lying is practiced to perfection, there may be little recordable difference in emotion as these liars recount events truthfully or falsely. These possibilities have led Lykken (1979) to bet that he can train guilty suspects to beat the polygraph.

Self-Deceivers

The most common form of deception is probably that committed against one's self. Psychotherapists in particular, but lay persons in general, judge people as more or less "insightful." People who lack "insight" are those who seem unable to recognize what they do and how others interpret their acts. They are deemed to be less objective about themselves and to "kid themselves" more frequently than do individuals who are more "true to themselves."

The assumption that people can deceive themselves rests on the premise that mental activity is *not* all of one piece, with every "piece" equally available to an individual's recognition. Consciousness *is* divided, as Hilgard (1977) demonstrates, and as psychoanalysts have long assumed. This means that individuals can differ in the quality and quantity of perceived information that they repress. The idea of repression is the notion that individuals *selectively* appreciate what they have perceived, that selective awareness and "forgetting" are motivated, and that individuals differ in their abilities to report what has happened to them, how they feel, and, in short, "who they are." Self-deception is a necessary element in repression although it does not cover all that psychoanalysts mean by the term. What is of moment to criminologists, however, is the probability that the tendency to deceive one's self is a "generalized response set" (Hilgard 1949, Meehl & Hathaway 1946). It is a personality characteristic, particularly notable among persons called "neurotic" (Abramson & Sackeim 1977, Mischel 1974).

The utility of the idea of self-deception is demonstrated by measurement of the phenomenon. Gur and Sackeim (1979) report measures of self-deception that fulfill four criteria of this activity:

1. The individual holds two contradictory beliefs.
2. These two contradictory beliefs are held simultaneously.
3. The individual is not aware of holding one of the beliefs.
4. The act that determines which belief is, or is not, subject to awareness is a motivated act (p. 149).

Gur and Sackeim test for self-deception by asking subjects to identify their own and others' voices. They show that a measure of emotional response (the GSR) is *independent* of self-reports which are the usual signs of "awareness." They are then able to study the personalities and the contingencies associated with greater and lesser recognition of self and with greater and lesser *division* of the self between what is recorded by the physiological system and what can be reported by the individual.

Demonstration of self-deception is important for criminologists. First, it confirms skepticism of self-reports of activities, and particularly those activities that may be repressed like crimes and psychopathological feelings (Sackeim & Gur 1979). Second, it suggests limits to the utility of "understanding" others by listening to their reasons and other descriptions of themselves, as discussed in Chapter 2, Volume One.[9] Third, the possibility that people deceive themselves, and do so as a characteristic of their personalities, qualifies the truthfulness of witnesses. It also reminds us that some innocent individuals can be led to confess to acts they have *not* committed.

SUMMARY

Detecting deception is required work, whether it is done vocationally or avocationally. For the reasons discussed, it is work that can

---

[9] To give a reason is, of course, to describe oneself.

never be accomplished without error. How much error we can afford by trusting or not trusting is a function of each individual's resources. Life without trust is no fun; life with complete trust is dangerous. The best advice is Mr. Dooley's: "Thrust ivrybody, but cut th' ca-ards" (Dunne 1901).

Dooley's advice pertains particularly to the protection of societies against treason, the subject of the next chapter.

2 TREASON

Abstract • Treason is one of the oldest and most strongly condemned wrongs. ∘ Its definition rests on the necessity of sovereign defense. ∘ This necessity struggles with the desire for free expression and action. ∘ Reconciling these necessities is difficult politically. It is also difficult philosophically because treason and related deceits are crimes most fortified by moral justification. ∘ Appeal to individual conscience as guide does not resolve the tension between the need for loyalty and the need to criticize. • Definition of treason rests on the duty of allegiance. ∘ The content of American, Canadian, and British laws against treason is outlined. ∘ Accessories to treason are guilty of treason. ∘ Misprision of treason is a crime. ∘ Degrees of treasonable activity are recognized in degrees of punishment allowed. ∘ Related crimes of disloyalty are sabotage, espionage, and sedition. • Varied routes to treason are described. ∘ Individual and collective avenues are noted. ∘ Some individual paths are traced in psychopathy, failure, and blackmail. ∘ The main road to treason turns alienation into idealism. Idealism is organized by ideology. • The meeting of personality with ideology is described. ∘ Two major ideologies are noted as contributors to treason in the Western world during the 20th century. ∘ Fascist and Communist ideals are compared. ∘ A sample of spies and traitors in Western countries is listed to indicate their personal diversity and generally high social status. • Lessons are deduced from the chronicle of treason and espionage: ∘ We cannot detect spies and traitors by their appearance. ∘ It is a mistake to think of political idealism as necessarily altruistic. Much of it is fueled by hate. ∘ Persons responsible for the security of their countries need to balance trust with suspicion. Some signs that should trigger suspicion are noted.

"POLITE LIES" ARE THOSE THAT DECEIVE NO ONE and therefore harm no one. Other deceptions, by definition, hurt. Within the circle of harmful deceit, many crimes reside but, of these, the most serious is that called *treason.*

Treason is one of the oldest and most strongly condemned wrongs. It is, for example, the *only* crime defined in the United States Constitution (article III, section 3).

The idea of treason rests on the necessity of self-defense. All aggregates of human beings that attempt to govern themselves defend their order-of-things against external and internal challenge. This fact pertains to aggregates as disparate as tribes and modern sovereign states. Loyalty is a necessity of social life.

This requirement confronts other values and it does so particularly in open societies. Allegiance is a requirement that is apt to be in conflict with curiosity, for example, and with the wish to explore, discuss, and criticize. It is a requirement that draws limits to free speech and the communication of ideas and information. Allegiance struggles with dissent.

Loyalty to a governing power is therefore a necessity that taxes legislators. Law-makers in free societies walk a fine line between protecting liberty and allowing license. It is this difficult balance that provokes most of the litigation concerning treason and related crimes of "civil disobedience."

Treason is a crime that also taxes philosophers because *disloyalty to a sovereign state is characteristically justified as moral conduct.* Treason is sometimes the crime of mercenaries and of disturbed persons. But it is normally the crime of persons of favorable repute who hold themselves to be moved only by the desire to do good. Traitors generally do not consider themselves to be wrong-doers.

Deception for Good Causes

We have, then, an interesting polarity. It is that, while treason and its related deceptions are codified as the most serious of crimes, and while such disloyalty potentially damages more people more grievously than do common lying, cheating, and stealing, yet *the traitorous mode of deceit is the one most fortified by moral justification.*

This fact clouds study of treason because the goodness of traitors' justifications intrudes upon evaluation of their criminality. All traitors have supporters—even within their own countries. Support begins by denying evidence of the deed. If such evidence appears incontrovertible, advocacy then shifts to deny the criminality of the treason. This denial, in turn, rests on arguments jointly condemning the present order and praising the intentions of the disloyal.

The final appeal in justification of treason is to "individual conscience." Some Western moralists elevate individual conscience to the role of supreme arbiter, superior to moral (that is, group) dictates.[1] Thus, in the disturbances within intellectual forums that followed conviction of America's most distinguished perjurer, Alger

---

[1] The notion of an "individual morality" is a contradiction. The word "morality" has Latin roots referring to the customs of a group.

Whether, and when, an individual should resist his tribe's practices is one of the most difficult questions for philosophers of right action.

Hiss, the literary critic Leslie Fiedler (1951) believed that a confession of conscience would excuse treasonous acts. Fiedler writes:

> Had [Hiss] been willing to say, 'Yes, I did these things—things it is now possible to call 'treason'—not for money or prestige, but out of a higher allegiance than patriotism'—had he only confessed . . . then he need not even have gone to prison. Why did he lie?

Joan Didion (1978, pp. 161–162) reminds us that many madmen, murderers, and traitors have claimed exemption from criminality by pleading, "I did what I thought was right." The "ethic of conscience," Didion concludes, "is intrinsically insidious." It leads to the "contradictory position that [following one's conscience] is dangerous when it is 'wrong,' and admirable when it is 'right'."

Evaluating disloyalty that is justified by appeal to a "higher allegiance" is difficult. Taking sides in particular cases leaves nothing to discuss other than one's preference for a present security or a promised better way.

The present resolution is to examine treason and traitors within the context of the laws of Western countries. Critics will consider, of course, whether those laws are good ones and whether Western civilization deserves such defense. These are issues for other texts. But, whatever one thinks of the laws defining allegiance to a present Western state, there is no escaping some such law. To repeat, all governing bodies attempt to maintain loyalty and they condemn those disloyalties that are deemed to threaten the group's security.

DEFINITIONS

The United States and countries of the British Commonwealth of Nations have adopted definitions of treason and related crimes from the *English Statute of Treasons* passed during the reign of King Edward III (1327–1377). The objectives of this legislation were to *reduce* the number of offenses that could be prosecuted as traitorous and to require that an *overt act* be committed for such a charge to be laid.

Allegiance

The heart of treason is "a breach of allegiance to a government committed by a person who owes allegiance to it" (Schiffres 1973, p. 7, §4).

Those who owe allegiance are citizens of the state, whether they reside at home or abroad. In their case, allegiance is absolute. However, allegiance is also deemed to be local and temporary and it applies, then, to aliens whose loyalty is expected in return for the protection received while domiciled in the host country.

Content

With some variation by jurisdiction, countries whose laws against treason and related crimes have evolved out of English law condemn as treason the following acts:

1. Levying war against the homeland or preparing to do so.

2. "Adhering" to the homeland's enemies, giving them "aid and comfort." In Canada this includes assisting "... any armed forces against whom Canadian Forces are engaged in hostilities whether or not a state of war exists. . . ." (Martin & Cartwright 1978, p. 33, §46c).

In the United States, "aid and comfort" are given whenever:

> overt acts are committed which, in their natural consequence, if successful, would encourage and advance the interests of the enemy. The term "aid and comfort" as used in this provision, contemplates some kind of affirmative action, deed, or physical activity tending to strengthen the enemy or weaken the power to resist him, and is not satisfied by a mere mental operation. The term "enemies" within the meaning of this clause means the subjects of a foreign power in open hostility with the United States (Schiffres 1973, p. 39, §50).

3. Using "force or violence" to overthrow federal, state, or provincial government.

4. Providing a foreign agent information of a military or scientific character (including sketches, plans, models, articles, notes, or documents) that a citizen knows, or ought to know, may be used by the foreign state in a manner "prejudicial to the safety or defense" of the homeland.

5. Conspiring to do any of the acts condemned in paragraphs 1–4 above. It is also treasonous if one *intends* to do any of those prohibited acts *if* the intention is manifested by an *overt act*.

6. To this content of treasons, Canadian law adds:

> ... kills or attempts to kill Her Majesty, or does her any bodily harm tending to death or destruction, maims or wounds her, or imprisons or restrains her (Martin & Cartwright 1978, p. 33, §46a).

And British law adds such treasons as:

(a) compasses or imagines the death of the Sovereign;

(b) compasses or imagines the death of the King's wife or of the Sovereign's eldest son and heir;

(c) violates the King's wife or the Sovereign's eldest daughter un-married or the wife of the Sovereign's eldest son and heir;

(d) slays the Chancellor, Treasurer, or the King's justices, being in their places, doing their offices (Hailsham 1976, p. 478, §811).

Accessories

The gravity accorded the crime of treason is indicated by the fact that for this indictable offense, in contrast with other felonies, *there can be no accessories.* While, in the case of other serious crimes, one can be charged with the lesser offense of aiding the crime *without* participating in its commission, this exemption does *not* apply to trai-torous acts. As Schiffres (1973, p. 35, §44) puts it, ". . . all who play a part, however minute, or however remote from the place of action, and who are leagued in the general conspiracy, are guilty of treason."

Misprision

Misprision (pronounced mis-PRIZH-un) is a crime of omission. It is the failure of a person not actively engaged in a crime either to pre-vent its occurrence or, having knowledge of the crime, to report it to lawful authorities.

American law defines misprision of treason by extending the meaning of treason to include concealing conspiracy to commit this crime or failing to disclose it. Canadian law treats misprision of trea-son in a section separate from treason itself as a crime intended "to alarm Her Majesty or break the public peace."

Punishment

Degrees of treasonable activity are recognized and, hence, sen-tences may vary. Western countries allow the death penalty for spe-cific qualities of treason. Killing or attempting to kill the head of state, levying war against the homeland or preparing to do so, assisting an enemy at war with one's country, and assisting armed forces with whom one's country is "engaged in hostilities" with, or without, a declaration of war make one liable to the death penalty.

In the United States, courts may commute the death sentence to a term of imprisonment. However, "a reviewing court is *not* warranted in interfering with a death sentence where the defendant has committed flagrant and persistent acts of treason" (Schiffres 1973, p. 43, §56, emphasis added).

Related Crimes

Varieties of treason are associated in principle with other qualities of threat to the security of a state. The wording of the law differs somewhat with jurisdiction, but all modern states condemn as crimes the following:

1. Sabotage   Those acts of omission or commission that are intended to weaken the security and defense of a country. Such acts may destroy military equipment or any other property deemed necessary for national defense. Activities are also considered to be sabotage if they are designed to reduce productive efficiency in work essential for defense.

2. Espionage   The unauthorized gathering and transmission of information to foreign powers where such information is deemed confidential in the protection of national security. In Canada this crime is punished under the law of treason. In the United States a separate Espionage Act defines this crime and permits the death penalty. As with other treasonous acts, *conspiracy* to commit espionage and *misprision* of espionage are also crimes.

3. Sedition   The crime of inciting rebellion against a government. What constitutes illegal incitement changes as governments feel themselves to be more or less threatened.

The purpose of laws against sedition is to prohibit conspiracies, teachings, and propaganda that advocate, in the words of the Canadian law, "the use, without authority of law, of force as a means of accomplishing a governmental change" (Martin & Cartwright 1978, p. 38, §60). In common law, sedition meant:

> . . . acts done, words spoken and published or writings published with a seditious intention, that is an intention (1) to bring into hatred or contempt, or to excite disaffection against, the Sovereign or the government and consitution of the United Kingdom, or either House of Parliament, or the administration of justice; or (2) to excite the Sovereign's subjects to attempt, otherwise than by lawful means, the alteration of any matter in church or state by law established; or (3) to incite persons to commit any crime in general disturbance of the peace; or (4) to raise discontent or disaffection among the Sovereign's subjects; or (5) to promote feelings of ill-will and hostility between different classes of those subjects. An intention is not seditious if the object is to show that the Sovereign has

been misled or mistaken in her measures, or to point out errors or defects in the government or constitution with a view to their reformation, or to excite the subjects to attempt by lawful means the alteration of any matter in church or state by law established, or to point out, with a view to their removal, matters which are producing, or have a tendency to produce, feelings of hatred and ill-will between classes of the Sovereign's subjects (Hailsham 1976, §827).

The difficulty with laws against sedition and subversion is that open societies wish to permit criticism of legislation and administration without at the same time incurring the risk that such criticism will produce acts, including speech and publication, intended to stimulate armed overthrow of the government. Attempting to strike this difficult balance has led the United States to a variety of anti-sedition laws. The original Sedition Law of 1798 called for punishment:

> ... of any person who published any false and malicious thing against the Government of the United States, or any matter intended to excite the people to oppose any law, or any act of the President in pursuance of law, or to resist, oppose, or defeat any law.
>
> Thus, when President John Adams, while passing through Newark, New Jersey, was greeted by the firing of a cannon, a bystander said, "There goes the President and they are firing at his ass." One Baldwin replied that he did not care "if they fired through his ass," and was convicted for speaking "seditious words tending to defame the President and Government of the United States."
>
> The Sedition Act was never tested in the United States Supreme Court but it was vigorously condemned as unconstitutional in an attack joined in by Jefferson and Madison (Schiffres 1973, p. 11, §10).

The Sedition Act expired in 1801, but it has been replaced with a series of laws intended to protect the United States against advocacy of violent change of government. World War I produced a spate of such legislation, some of which was repealed in the 1920s. World War II bred a new generation of laws against sedition and subversion.

A major difference between British and Canadian legislation and American law in the control of sedition is that United States law defines Communist activities and the Communist Party as:

> ... an instrumentality of a conspiracy to overthrow the Government of the United States. [It holds the Communist Party to be] an agency of a hostile foreign power [which] renders its existence a clear, present, and continuing danger to the security of the United States. [The Communist

Control Act of 1954] does not repeal the Smith Act of 1940 which deals with the direct promotion of treason and sedition.

The Communist Control Act provides that the Communist Party of the United States is not entitled to any of the rights, privileges, and immunities attendant upon legal bodies created under the jurisdiction of the laws of the United States. . . . it has been held that a candidate for public office can be barred from running under the Communist Party banner under this law.

The act further provides that whoever knowingly and wilfully becomes or remains a member of the Communist Party (or of any other group which has as one of its purposes the overthrow of the government by the use of force or violence) shall be subject to all the provisions and penalties of the Internal Security Act (Schiffres 1973, p. 32, §40).

ROADS TO TREASON AND RELATED CRIMES

Treason and related threats to a country's security are usually crimes of deceit. Perpetrators pretend to be what they are not and they conceal from some associates what they are.

As with other crimes, there are several roads to these deceits. The professional spy working for his or her own country is but another legitimate worker in a bureaucracy, comparable to a police person or, better, to a Special Services (SS) soldier. The attractions of this work include regular pay, episodic excitement, and the possibility of advancement.

This kind of legitimate career in deceit does not require the greater deception of illicit careers in disloyalty to one's own country. Traitors, and spies for foreign states, are led to their actions down a different course. A first step in these illegal careers involves *alienation* from the society to which one owes allegiance.

Alienation is variously produced, but it is recognizable as disaffection with the society of which one is a nominal part (Nettler 1957). Feelings of estrangement range in quality and intensity from resentment at failed ambitions in work and love, to dislike of the culture that surrounds one, to hatred of the economic and political arrangements with which one lives.

Alienation may have highly individual origins or the sources may be more collective and objective. Individual origins include personality variables. A classic beginning for the alienated person is reciprocated rejection: parents are less than enthusiastic about child, child returns the dislike, and dislike of these "first people" translates into misanthropy. It is no psychological contradiction, incidentally, to find that such wounded individuals develop a strong sense of injustice that applies to mankind in general without applying to persons in particular. In the alienated ones, rage at injustice is expressed in sympathy for the suffering of distant humankind, but without a complementary appreciation of the feelings of intimate others.

By contrast with such individual origins, collective and objective sources of estrangement refer to social conditions representing discontinuities with a past and with the expectations that past has built. An example is the widespread alienation stimulated in the Western world by the Great Depression of the 1930s. This estrangement was more objective, and less idiosyncratic, than many current disaffections. It was "objective" in that there was general agreement that "things were not working."

Such agreement functions as a moral atmosphere. The moral atmosphere includes *descriptions* of the breakdown and *prescriptions* for its cure. One kind of cure idealizes the "better arrangements" in a foreign land, and such idealization opens the door to traitorous conduct in favor of that alien country.

Individual and collective routes to treason cross. In any one career toward dangerous deceit there are blends of the subjective and the objective as causes of action. This allows the possibility that there are tributaries of personal character that feed into the main roads to treason.

One such tributary is that of intelligent psychopathy. There are persons who enjoy games of deception. They enjoy battles of wits as chess masters enjoy their challenges. But the psychopath's pleasure is in duping those who trust him.

For example, the British subject George Blake was convicted of five charges of espionage in 1961 and sentenced to 42 years in prison. While working for the Foreign Office he is alleged to have betrayed more than 50 NATO agents to the Communists. In 1966 Blake escaped from Wormwood Scrubs prison and fled to the Soviet Union where, in 1970, he received its second highest honor, the Order of Lenin. In his interview with the Soviet press, Blake described with pride how he had outfoxed his colleagues in the British Foreign Office. His abandoned wife, Gillian, who had lived for years with this man without knowing of his duplicity, could only explain him by saying that, "George liked to be a power behind the scenes. . . ." (Newman 1973, p. 165).

The "mystery" of such a person is best clarified by the novelist Balzac who once commented that "a spy is someone who craves the excitement of being a criminal while keeping the character of an honest man" (Newman 1973, p. 165).

Another side road leading to disloyalty is that of financial failure and debt. The lure here is reward for turning traitor—a salary and perquisites from a foreign state.

Yet another tributary is characterized by blackmail, where the blackmail may be subtle or strong. On this route the candidate for treason has been found out in, or led to, some scandal—sexual or financial. Recruiting agents for foreign countries—and there *are* such—use knowledge of the scandal as leverage. The leverage can be applied, of course, with some salving of the candidate's conscience by payments made to monetary banks or moral ones. The "moral bank" is that treasury of self-feeling that tells one that the deceitful action is moved by, and will do, good.

These personal by-ways toward treason are best summarized by Soviet General Pavl Sudoplatov, Director of the Special Bureau of the KGB (*Komitat Gosudarstvennoi Bezopastnosti,* see fn. 6), the Soviet security service. Sudoplatov advised one of his recruiters:

> Go search for people who are hurt by fate or nature—the ugly, those suffering from an inferiority complex, craving power and influence but defeated by unfavorable circumstances. . . . The sense of belonging to an influential, powerful organization will give them a feeling of superiority over the handsome and prosperous people around them. For the first time in their lives they will experience a sense of importance. . . . It is sad indeed, and humanly shallow—but we are obliged to profit from it (Barron 1974, p. 417).

Recruiters of traitors work like efficient sales people and con-artists. They assess others' vulnerability to a "pitch." Vulnerability is recognized by testing what the "pigeon" wants. The "sale" is then "pitched" to those appetites. Finding what motivates the prospect provides the key for "turning" him or her.[2]

The Main Road

The many tributaries that lead to careers in disloyalty tell us something, but not everything, about individual differences in vulnerability to treason. Personal defects and failed ambitions make one vulnerable, but these disabilities are too common to explain much in the selection process. After the fact of a major crime, we refer to these

[2] A training manual for Soviet recruiters of spies in the Americas and "Third Countries" is reprinted as an appendix in Barron's (1974) study of the KGB.

deficits as somehow crucial in a career. Before the fact, they have little premonitory power. Disabilities may work, of course, as contributors in a web of causes and, as such, they may lead to the main road to treason. This is the one marked by contingencies that *convert alienation into idealism.*

Conversion occurs as the estranged person meets people whose ideas and actions organize what troubles one into a system of propositions and attitudes that "make sense" of the world. It is, of course, one of the functions of religion to make sense of the many incongruities in our lives. When orthodox religions lose their powers, as they do for many alienated individuals, new religions are invented that perform the organizing function. In her study of treason, Dame Rebecca West (1964, pp. 119–120) describes the conversion this way:

> Those who have discarded the idea of a superpersonal God and still desire an enduring friendship must look for it in those fields of life farthest removed from ordinary personal relationship, because human personality lacks endurance in any form of love. The most obvious of these is politics. There a leader can excite love in followers who know nothing of him save his public appearances. That love is unqualified; for no party can cause its enemies to rejoice by admitting that its leader has any faults, and what parties profess they soon sincerely feel, especially in crowded halls. That love swears itself undying, too; for no party can afford to let itself be overheard contemplating the exchange of its leader for another.
>
> Therefore many men who would have been happy in the practice of religion during the ages of faith have in these modern times a need for participation in politics which is as strong as the need for food, for shelter, for sex. Such persons never speak of the real motives which impel them to their pursuit of politics, but continually refer, in accents of assumed passion, to motives which do indeed preoccupy some politicians, but not them. The chief of these is the desire to end poverty. But William Joyce [a traitor] had never in his life known what it was to be hungry or cold or workless, and he did not belong to the altruistic type which torments itself over the plight of others. . . . His was another hunger, another chill, another kind of unemployment. But the only people in the generation before him who attacked the governing class had been poor or altruist, and since their attack had been successful their vocabulary held a tang of victory, and William Joyce and his kind borrowed it.
>
> Therefore they spoke of economics when they were thinking of religion . . . in our day, those suffering from religious distress . . . complain of it in economic terms. Those who desire salvation pretend that they are seeking a plan to feed the hungry.

Ideology

Alienation is sometimes relieved by idealism. Idealism motivates action as its assumptions about the working of the world become patterned. The pattern consists of images, ideas, and related practices.[3] When the pattern yields a distinctive content of notions that make the ideals seem both justifiable and realizable, it constitutes an *ideology*.

Ideology is a word coined by the French philosopher-psychologist A.L.C. Destutt de Tracy (1754–1836). Destutt and his fellow *ideologues* regarded ideology as a means of cleansing thought of personal bias and superstition so that a "rational society" could be built on a foundation of knowledge.

Ideology today retains this reformist attitude, but its rational basis has been eroded. As the term is now used, ideology refers to a system of belief that masquerades values as facts (Bergmann 1968). Ideology consists of "intensely espoused value orientations which . . . transcend current reality by a wide margin, which are explicit, articulated, and hostile to the existing order" (Shils 1975, p. 5).

In the twentieth century two major ideologies have contested for revolutionary allegiance in opposition to democratic societies with their mixed economies and so-called "bourgeois" moralities. The two contestants have been called Fascism and Communism, although there are varieties of belief among adherents to both sets of ideals and striking parallels between the political poles commonly called Left and Right. Naziism, for example, is frequently mentioned as a kind of Fascism, and Marxist-Leninism prefers to distinguish itself from another brand of Communism, Trotskyism. However, while these families of ideology are at war among themselves, they share some common ground of belief,[4] and both have produced traitors, spies,

---

[3] Practice is an essential part of religious belief. It is expressed in ritual within churchly ceremonies and it extends to habits of costume, diet, tonsure, sexual relations, and other aspects of daily routine.

New religions, including ideologies, invent rituals. The practices revive belief and mark off one group's territory of difference from another's.

[4] The popular Communist assumptions listed on subsequent pages apply generally to a wide range of "collectivist," including Nazis and Fascists.

One verbal difference between the ideologies concerns what they say about the innate goodness of Man. Communists and Socialists espouse this assumption; Nazis, in particular, deny it. However, the difference in verbalized assumption between Communists and Nazis has not led to differences in practice. Adherents to both camps kill generically defined enemies, on principle, and they do so whether they define enemies by class or race.

Another difference is that Nazi-Fascist societies can be best characterized as *authoritarian* whereas Communist societies are better characterized as *to-*

assassins, and saboteurs. The production again illuminates the many paths a traitor's career may take.

Impotence Lusting for Power

A timeless road to treason guides lust for power in a person who is a nobody. To dream of power while recognizing one's own insignificance is insulting. The insult can be paid back by gaining power, by being in command, by being cheered and feared. Power compensates feelings of inferiority.

This route describes the career of the British traitor, William Joyce, known during World War II as "Lord Haw-Haw" for his treasonous broadcasts to England from Nazi Germany. Joyce was the son of British parents, born while they were visiting the United States. His birthplace gave him American citizenship, but Joyce spent his formative years in England where he was adequately schooled and comfortably reared.

Early on Joyce showed interest in command and in setting things aright by force. This is not an unusual characteristic. However, in the climate of the disorderly 1930s, and with models of successful Communist and Fascist revolutions before him, Joyce's interests fit nicely with a view of the world copied from Mussolini's authoritarianism. This view was being advanced in the British Isles by a handsome, intelligent, and rich baronet, Sir Oswald Mosley, who had suffered defeat and humiliation in his attempts to promote his own socialist party which was to have been more "drastic and dashing than the Labour Party" (West 1964, p. 47).

Having failed as a socialist, Mosley made the not uncommon swing from one dogma to another and formed the British Union of Fascists. Joyce became his Director of Propaganda. However, Joyce did not

---

talitarian. The distinction refers to zones of activity—religious, educational, agricultural, commercial, and industrial—that are left relatively free in authoritarian states, but commanded in totalitarian states.

Parallels in practices by ideologues assumed to be poles apart are so strong as to have led America's National Security Advisor Zbigniew Brzezinski (1969) to suggest that "recent developments in the Soviet Union seem to indicate that the highest stage of communism is fascism." In this vein, the political scientist A.J. Gregor (1974, p. 424) concludes that "fascist and communist regimes are subspecies of one and the same species."

Parallels are frequently seen in the careers of individual politicians. For example, Benito Mussolini, the first Fascist, began as an intellectual, a journalist, and a socialist. And we have seen that Mosley and Joyce embraced socialism on their roads to Fascism. We are reminded, too, that the word "Nazi" is a derisive abbreviation of the German words for National Socialist German Workers' Party (*Nationalsozialistische Deutsche Arbeiterpartei*).

get along well with Mosley. He felt cut off from the wealthy ring of Mosley's supporters who, Joyce knew, regarded him as "common." In addition, the Fascist Union suffered financial set-backs just as Joyce's financial needs increased as a consequence of divorce and re-marriage. As the prospects of war mounted in the summer of 1939, Joyce made plans to flee to Germany and offer his services to the Nazis. Two weeks after the declaration of war between England and Germany, Joyce began broadcasting for the English-language arm of German radio. He became a German citizen in 1940.

With the defeat of Germany in 1945, Joyce and his wife tried to es-cape into Denmark but were arrested, quite by accident, by two En-glish officers. Joyce was tried for high treason and hung. Defense counsel attempted to save him by arguing that Joyce was not a Brit-ish subject but, rather, that he was an American by birth and a Ger-man by naturalization. These facts are correct, but this defense failed because the law of treason applies to aliens residing in a state. The reasoning goes back to Sir Edward Coke's seventeenth century maxim, "Protection draws allegiance, and allegiance draws protection."

Communist Ideals

Revolutionaries of Fascist persuasion persist, but they are small in numbers and weak in powers compared with advocates of the Com-munist cause. An interesting feature of Communist appeal is that its professed ideology strikes a sympathetic chord in the world outlook of Western intellectuals and their followers. This makes Communist propaganda easier. It also makes Westerners vulnerable to crimes of disloyalty.

The idealism inspired by Communist ideology can be described as a bundle of assumptions. This description does not challenge the validity of all the premises. Since ideology masquerades values as facts, many of the premises are preferences that can be accepted or rejected, but not proved. However, as a schema for interpreting the world and its working, this ideology is persuasive, popular, and prophetically inaccurate. It does not deliver what it promises. Never-theless, in generating action, promises are sometimes more stimu-lating than realities.

The idealism that has made the greatest contribution to traitorous acts among Westerners includes the following assumptions, briefly presented:

1. The world is material. The realm of the supernatural is denied. In this sense, Communist ideology is *not* religious. But, in the sense of requiring faith and of operating as a faith immune to rebuttal, it *is* religious.

2. This ideology distrusts what it calls "the profit motive."[5]

It has confidence in the greater efficiency and justice of central planning of an economy as compared with the unplanned results of market allocation. It therefore prefers rationing by government edict to rationing by individual purchase.

3. This ideology believes that the best social arrangements are those enacted according to human design. It therefore denies the goodness of social arrangements that *evolve*.

A corollary of this assumption is belief that good results occur most frequently when they are *intended*. The goodness of *unintended* consequences is ignored, if not denied.

4. The ideal of equality of condition is preferred to the ideal of equality of opportunity.

The ideal of equal condition is not achieved, of course, but ideals can persist as motivants despite their shortfalls in reality (Matthews 1981, McAuley 1981, Yanowitch 1981).

5. Communist ideals assume that human beings are "basically good" and corrupted only by present institutions. Overthrowing these institutions and creating new ones will, it is promised, end poverty, inequality, war, and crime.

6. Communist ideology believes that its major enemy is consolidated and conspiratorial. Counter-conspiracy is therefore justified.

7. Bolsheviks like N. Lenin tended to be "hard-headed realists" who assumed that there was a real world that existed independently of one's knowledge of it or hopes for it. However, a "soft" epistemology characterizes the ideology of Communists and their Western sympathizers. In brief, this concept of knowledge holds that "consciousness" is determined by socio-economic position and that, therefore, attempts to be objective and scientific about one's social relations are always contaminated. It is claimed that such attempts serve as camouflage for "class interests."

The "politics of reality" deserves more attention than can be given here. We can note only that the revolutionary position disdains science in favor of phenomenology. It prefers "personal knowledge" to public knowledge (Evola 1930, 1934) and holds, with Robert Young (1973), that the concepts of "objectivity" and "truth" constitute "a colossal confidence trick." This ideology favors evaluating truth by

---

[5] The "profit motive" is not a clear concept. Derivative ideas like "exploitation" and "unearned income" are equally confused. Anthony Flew (1976) describes some of the misconceptions.

preferred consequences and it infuses fact with value. In the words of the popular teacher Herbert Marcuse (1964), "Epistemology is in itself ethics and ethics is epistemology."

This is the epistemology of hope. It is a theory of knowledge that cannot be maintained consistently. At some point, a real world is assumed even by those who hold that reality is only "socially constructed." Without the assumption of our ability tremblingly to ascertain facts, and to discriminate between facts and desires, no proposition could be justified, including propositions of this ideology (see assumptions #2 above and #9 below, for example). Without a real world to be known independently of our wishes, silence would be the only reasonable recourse in debate.

8. Communist ideology believes, with one of its instructors, Lenin, that "the people" do not know what is good for them and that leaders, with "the best interests of the masses" at heart, will have to "midwife History."

9. Communist ideology conceives History as an inevitable process, governed by "laws" which it knows.

The historical process is believed to unravel in ineluctable stages and to guarantee the correctness of its ideals. A consequence of these beliefs is denial of lessons from the past, no love for the present, but hope for the future.

Conversion

Communist beliefs are idealistic in the sense that they urge action to move from a bad state of affairs to a better one. The idealism of the ideology makes it popular. Its popularity, in turn, makes it difficult to identify spies and traitors among those who espouse such common assumptions. Identification is made additionally difficult because this road to crime is the one most heavily traveled by intellectuals.

Detailing this route should not lead to the conclusion that every advocate of the described ideology is at high risk of espionage and sedition. The correction for such all-or-none thinking is given in Chapter 3, Volume One, where the difference between the validity of cues and their predictive accuracy is diagrammed (Table 3.1 and Figure 3.2).

Given a large library of beliefs from which to choose, personalities *select* political beliefs as they do other preferences, and they select them with differing degrees of commitment to the actions the ideas suggest. Ideas do not fill people as though they were empty vessels.

William James (1907) noted that temperaments select philosophies. We can add that temperaments change environments and differentially interact with them (Cattell 1980). We have only poor measures of these processes, but James's thesis advises us that both the selection of ideologies and commitment to their practice vary with personality and situation. The *need* to believe, and the *consistency* with which ideas are transformed into actions, are personality traits.

Turning into the road toward treason is accomplished by converting uncompensated and emotionalized alienation into compensating and gratifying idealistic action. The need for such action resides in personalities. The conversion is provided by associates.

This is the course followed by most of the Western world's spies and traitors during and since the second World War. The roster of such careerists is international and large. The social status and intellectual standing of these deceivers can be noted from the following, abbreviated list. Positions refer to those held at the time of their apprehension:

In Canada: Eric Adams, a graduate in engineering and business administration, served on the Wartime Requirements Board, the Foreign Exchange Control Board, the Bank of Canada, and the Industrial Development Bank. He was secretary of the Main Examining Committee of the Inventions Board during the war and, under the cover name, "Ernst," transmitted secret documents to the Soviet Union.

J.S. Benning worked in the Department of Munitions and Supply from which he funneled at least 70 secret documents to Russian agents.

Dr. Raymond Boyer, an internationally renowned scientist. He was an expert on explosives and a senior member of the National Research Council. He helped develop a new explosive, RDX, the plans for which he transmitted to the Soviet Embassy.

David Gordon Lunan, editor of *Canadian Affairs* and captain in the Canadian Information Services. He served as liaison between scientists in the National Research Council and Soviet agents, passing secret information from one to the other.

Dr. Allan Nunn May, atomic physicist. He was tried in England for espionage, 1946, and sentenced to ten years in prison.

Dr. David Shugar, physicist. He worked for Research Enterprises, a Crown corporation engaged in radar and anti-submarine technology. He was later an officer in the Canadian navy and an official in the Directorate of Electrical Supply. He was charged with violations of the Official Secrets Act.

Dunford Smith, an honors graduate in mathematics and physics from McGill University and an officer in the National Research Council. He transmitted secret documents on radar research to the Soviet Union and was convicted of conspiracy in espionage.

Suspects   Suspicion of treason has followed the careers of other prominent Canadians. In 1945, Igor Gouzenko, a cipher clerk, defected from the Soviet embassy in Ottawa and exposed a network of spies operating for Russia in Canada, England, and the United States. Gouzenko's information, and later revelations from one of the "Cambridge Four" (this chapter), suggest that the former Canadian ambassador to Egypt, Herbert Norman, and the former Canadian chargé d'affaires ad interim in the Soviet Union, John Watkins, may both have served the instructions of the Soviet Union.

Norman was allegedly recruited during his student days in England by a university don, Anthony Blunt. CIA advice alerted Canadian authorities to Norman's possible connections with the KGB and he was asked to return to Ottawa for questioning. Rather than return to Canada where, he is reported to have said, "I would have to betray more than a hundred people," Norman killed himself by leaping from the roof of his Cairo apartment building (Pincher 1981, p. 139).

Watkins was allegedly blackmailed into service for the KGB after the Russians had claimed to have photographed him in homosexual relations during his Moscow assignment. Watkins was returned to Ottawa for interrogation, but he died of a heart attack before inquiry could be completed.

Norman and Watkins were friends of the then Canadian Prime Minister, Lester Pearson, and investigators today claim that "party politics" continues to conceal the extent of these diplomats' deceits (Farran 1981, Jackson 1981).

In France: Dmitri Volokov, atomic-energy engineer. He confessed in 1971 to having been a Soviet agent for more than a decade.

In Italy: Giorgio Rinaldi, antique dealer (Turin) and sporting skydiver. Rinaldi used his participation in international skydiving events to recruit spies from Somalia to Scandinavia. Western intelligence observed his meetings with Soviet agents and in 1967 Rinaldi confessed to espionage (Newman 1973, pp. 175–176).

In Sweden: Colonel Stig Wennerström, Swedish Air Force. He was charged with stealing U.S. and NATO military secrets for transmission to the USSR and sentenced to prison for life (Barron 1974, p. 256).

In West Germany: Dr. Josef Eitzenberger, mathematician. He was arrested in 1968 for transmitting military data to the USSR. Eitzenberger had been entrusted with development of an "unbreakable" code to be used by NATO command. He admitted having been a KGB agent for at least ten years prior to his arrest.

In Great Britain: Dr. Klaus Fuchs, atomic physicist. He was one of the Soviet Union's most important spies, a man who transmitted American, Canadian, and British secrets on atomic power to the Communists and thus allowed them to develop the atom bomb years before their own scientists could have done so. Fuchs was not "turned into" a spy by "pressure" or bribery. He offered his services to the Soviet Union because of his faith in an ideology and his conceit that he knew how to make the world a better place.

Fuchs's allegiance to the Soviet Union was well known during the time he worked on nuclear projects on both sides of the Atlantic. Despite his avowed Communism and the enthusiasm with which he praised the Soviet Union and sang Russian songs at scientists' parties, he was not suspected of being a security risk (Franklin 1967). When he left work on the Los Alamos atom bomb project in 1946, the security department there gave him an enthusiastic recommendation that helped gain him a position as head of the theoretical division of the British Atomic Energy Centre.

Revelation of a Soviet spy ring in Canada and the United States led to British investigation of Fuchs. Clever detective work broke Fuch's silence and produced a confession. He was not charged with treason, for which the penalty could have been death, but with transmission of secret information. He was sentenced to 14 years in prison and deprived of his British citizenship. Upon his release in 1959 Fuchs moved to East Germany where he holds the post of Deputy Director of the Control Institute for Nuclear Research. As with other faithful spies, Fuchs believes he did right and that he has nothing to repent.

Bruno Pontecorvo, nuclear physicist: Pontecorvo was born in Pisa, Italy, of a prosperous family. He was a brilliant student who earned his doctorate in physics at the University of Rome when he was 21 years old. Pontecorvo continued in the University, teaching, and conducting research with Enrico Fermi, one of the luminaries in theoretical physics. In 1936 Pontecorvo earned a fellowship that allowed him to work in Paris in the Institute of Radium with the Nobel prize-winning chemists-physicists, Frédéric and Irène Joliot-Curie.

The Joliot-Curies were dedicated members of the Communist Party. Frédéric became chairman of France's atomic energy commission, but was forced to resign in 1950 because of his political activity. He later became a member of the French Communist Party's Central Committee.

Pontecorvo's after-work companions were similarly of the Left. He became closely acquainted in Paris with Donald Maclean, one of Britain's more famous traitors (pp. 54-55), and took up residence with

Helene Marianne Nordblom, a Swedish Communist, who bore him a son in 1938. In 1940, Nordblum and Pontecorvo were married.

In addition to these affiliations, Pontecorvo's Italian family, exclusive of his parents, were heavily invested in Communism. His brother, Gilberto, was active in Communist Party politics, was tried once for sedition, and acquitted. His sister, Giuliana, married Duccio Tabet, a Party functionary, and his cousin, Emilio Sereni, became a member of the Italian CP's Central Committee.

Despite this network of intimates of dubious loyalty, Pontecorvo's brilliance won him clearance for secret research in Canada, the United States, and England. He worked for six years, 1943 to 1949, at Canada's heavy-water installation at Chalk River. He became a British subject in 1948 after interviews with security officers who either did not know, or saw no significance in, Pontecorvo's Communist relatives and friends.

In 1949, Pontecorvo went to work in England's atomic research station at Harwell, turning down higher-paying posts offered by Cornell University and the General Electric Company. Since Pontecorvo had always expressed a love of money, it is assumed that he took the lower-paying, confidential post under Soviet instruction (Toledano 1977).

In 1950, Pontecorvo and his family fled to Russia from holiday in Italy. Eight years later, Pontecorvo received the Lenin Prize for designing a ten-billion volt atomic particle accelerator.

No one knows how much classified information Pontecorvo transmitted to the Soviet Union prior to his defection, but one of the greatest losses to the West is his brains.

The "Cambridge Four": Anthony Blunt, Guy Francis de Moncy Burgess, Donald Maclean, Harold Adrian Russell (Kim) Philby. The careers of these four spies entwined faith in Communism with high office in the homeland and disloyalty to it.

All four men attended Trinity College, Cambridge University, where they acquired Communism. All four, at various times, held positions of trust and worked for British Intelligence.

Philby worked for years as a spy for the British, but he was all the while loyal to the Communists and filtering them information. Maclean moved in the highest echelons of the Foreign Office. He served in the British Embassy in Washington, D.C., while hating the Americans. At one time he was Head of the American Department in the Foreign Office and Secretary to the Atomic Energy Committee.

Burgess broadcast for the BBC, worked in the private office of the Minister of State in the Foreign Office, and was posted to the British

Embassy in Washington where his rude and drunken behavior got him suspended and shipped home in disgrace.

Blunt was a Cambridge Don who became Surveyor of the King's and, later, Queen's pictures. He was Director of the Courtauld Institute of Art and Commander in the Order of Orange Nassau. He served in British Intelligence during World War II, was knighted in 1956, and awarded the French Légion d'Honneur in 1958.

In 1951 Burgess and Maclean disappeared to surface in Moscow five years later. Burgess died there in 1963; Maclean still lives there, an unhappy exile.

Philby's connections with Burgess and Maclean led to his interrogation in 1951 and questions in the House of Commons in 1955. The Prime Minister defended Philby, but he was dismissed from his post with MI$_6$, the sixth section of British Military Intelligence, now the Secret Service (SIS). It was not until 1962 that a chain of events exposed Philby as a KGB[6] agent while he was on assignment in the Near East. Philby escaped to Russia where he assumed citizenship, received the Red Banner of Honor (1965), and was promoted to general in the KGB (1979).

During investigation of these three traitors, there were hints that their ring of deceivers included other prominent Britons suspected, but not yet exposed. Blunt was one of the suspects and investigation of him began as early as 1951. Surveillance and interrogation continued during the 1950s, but it was not until 1964 that Blunt allegedly confessed his guilt to British Intelligence under promise of immunity from prosecution. In 1979, the Prime Minister named Blunt as the fourth man in the spy circle. The Queen withdrew Blunt's knighthood. He continues to live in England.

Climate of Treason   Boyle's (1979) study of the "Cambridge Connection" is rightly titled *The Climate of Treason.*[7] The careers of the Cambridge Four illustrate the operation of a moral atmosphere.

These men were spoiled in the Ortegan sense. As children and youths, they had been given privileges which were unearned and which seemed to them to be "the natural order of things" rather than the product of an evolving civilization. They matured in depressed times between two major wars. Their brief pasts and premonitions of

---

[6] KGB stands for *Komitat Gosudarstvennoi Bezopastnosti,* Committee for State Security of the Council of Ministers of the Soviet Union. KGB is comparable to the American FBI and CIA combined.

[7] Boyle's book, published in 1979 in England with the title *The Climate of Treason,* appeared in the United States in 1980 with its title changed to *The Fourth Man.* The English title is more descriptive.

their futures gave them no confidence in the governing processes of their country. They were schooled in disaffection with the social order of their homeland and vulnerable to stories that pictured a better world in the making abroad. They recruited and reinforced one another. Secrecy lent excitement to their work. Impatience with the evil they saw, but did not experience, allowed them to embrace evil as a corrective.

By all reports, the survivors among them are not penitent. Their lack of remorse tells of the armor that ideology provides.

The effects of a moral atmosphere are apparent, too, in the generation of America's more notable traitors.

In the United States: Nelson C. Drummond, Navy yeoman. While stationed in London he supplied Navy secrets to the USSR. Barron (1974, p. 356) reports that, "The United States had to spend $200 million revising plans, procedures, and manuals he compromised. The damage was judged so serious that Drummond was sentenced to life imprisonment."

Lt. Colonel William H. Whalen, U.S. Army, until 1981 the only American officer ever charged with spying for the Soviet Union. Whalen had retired at age 46 after 20 years of "distinguished service" and, at the time of his retirement, had been working as an intelligence aide to the Joint Chiefs of Staff. Observation of his meetings with Soviet Embassy officers led to his surveillance and arrest. He was charged with supplying the Russians with "information pertaining to atomic weaponry, missiles, military plans for the defense of Europe, information concerning the retaliation plans of the United States Strategic Air Command, and information pertaining to troop movements, documents, and writings relating to the national defense of the United States" (Newman, 1973, p. 174). He was sentenced to 15 years in prison.

Ethel and Julius Rosenberg, convicted in 1951 of wartime espionage and executed. Julius was an engineer with the U.S. Army Signal Corps. With his wife's help, he began transmitting military information to Soviet agents during the 1930s. The value of this information increased when Julius's brother-in-law, *David Greenglass,* became an employee at the Los Alamos atomic bomb project and was recruited to pass top-secret data on nuclear weaponry to the Rosenbergs. Greenglass turned "state's evidence" against the Rosenbergs and was given a 15 year prison term (Pilot 1952).

The Rosenbergs are the only United States civilians to have been executed for treason.

Alger Hiss, graduate of Harvard Law School, protegé of Professor (later Justice) Felix Frankfurter, law clerk for Justice Oliver Wendell

Holmes, Jr. Hiss went to work for large law firms engaged in corporate affairs, but his wife engaged him in "social causes" avocationally. The company he kept days was much different, ideologically, from the company he kept nights. In 1936 he took a post with the Department of State. He attended the Yalta Conference with Messrs. Churchill, Roosevelt, and Stalin, and became Director of the State Department's Office of Special Political Affairs with responsibility for United Nations business. He was Secretary General of the founding conference of the United Nations in San Francisco, 1945, and, after his State Department post, became President of the Carnegie Endowment for International Peace.

Never has a person of more distinguished credentials been accused of being a traitor.

In the late 1940s Whittaker Chambers, a former Communist and editor of *Time* magazine, accused Hiss of having been a Communist and a spy who stole documents from the Department of State. Hiss denied ever having been a Communist, having known Chambers, and, of course, having been a spy. After two trials, Hiss was convicted on two counts of perjury and sentenced to five years in prison on each count, the sentences to be served concurrently.

Hiss's vocational background, his enmity with Richard Nixon, and his alliance with "liberal"[8] causes have stimulated books and articles in his defense for the three decades since his trials. In 1978 historian Allen Weinstein published the results of a five-year study of the Hiss-Chambers case under the title, *Perjury.* Weinstein began his research with the assumption that Hiss was innocent. His investigation was aided considerably by access to FBI records obtained under a Freedom of Information Act. Weinstein's detailed analysis of the evidence

---

[8] "Liberal" is in quotation marks because it is another of our abused terms. Classical liberalism developed in the late eighteenth and nineteenth centuries. It was based on faith in progress and the essential goodness of Man. It assumed that intelligence will produce steady reform of the *status quo.* This liberalism defended the individual against powers of Church and State. It was pacifist and anti-imperialist. It approved of *laissez faire* economics, that is, market determination of production and distribution.

Twentieth century liberalism has turned 180 degrees from the nineteenth century liberal's desire to limit state power. The quality of "liberty" defended by these two liberalisms differs. Twentieth century liberals look to strong government to guarantee welfare and manage the economy. They favor state intervention in agriculture, commerce, manufacturing, education, and medical care. They favor government provision of a broad range of "social services." Twentieth century liberalism differs from Socialism and Communism principally in preferring equality of opportunity to equality of condition imposed by state control. This distinction is often blurred.

led him to reverse his initial opinion and to conclude that Hiss had been fairly tried and was guilty as charged.

LESSONS

We learn some lessons from these varied biographies of deceit:

1. We cannot detect spies and traitors by their appearance. The preceding chapter mentioned efforts to detect deception and listed some folk maxims about the likely appearance of a cheater. These maxims fail when applied to the masks worn by Big Deceivers.

For example, Hiss's accuser, Whittaker Chambers, looked like "an unmade bed." By contrast, Hiss was the model of probity—handsome, upright, and well-groomed. Mrs. Eleanor Roosevelt, wife of the former President of the United States, wrote in her newspaper column that, "All we need to do is to look at the two men to tell who is speaking the truth" (cited by Hook 1978, p. 49).

The same kind of error was committed by a prominent psychiatrist and a famous psychologist. The psychiatrist, Dr. Carl Binger, volunteered his services in Hiss's defense. He attempted to "analyze" the accuser, Chambers, in order to testify as an authority on Chambers's mental stability and veracity. Binger conducted his "examination" of Chambers by sitting in the courtroom, stenographer's pad in hand, staring intently at the witness, and taking notes (Weinstein 1978, p. 418). From these observations, and from reading Chambers's writing, Binger diagnosed Chambers as a psychopath given to pathological lying. One of the confirming signs of Chambers's psychopathy, according to the psychiatrist, was:

> Chambers's tendency on the witness chair to gaze up at the ceiling frequently. One of Murphy's [the prosecutor's] assistants had counted Binger staring in that direction fifty times in fifty-nine minutes, and the prosecutor asked if this constituted such symptoms as the doctor ascribed to Chambers. "Not alone," came the irritated response (Weinstein 1978, p. 489).

The prosecuting attorney, Thomas F. Murphy, made short work of debunking this "expert testimony." Murphy showed, among other things, that Binger had no norms for lying that would permit one to say how much lying constituted psychopathy and how much reformist soul-searching constituted psychic illness. Similarly, Murphy rebutted the testimony of Harvard psychologist, Henry A. Murray, father of the Thematic Apperception Test (TAT), who also diagnosed Chambers as a psychopath. Among the sillier of the cues Murray cited as indicative of "mental instability" was Chambers's conversion from the Episcopalian church to the Quaker faith (Weinstein 1978, p. 493).

2. It is a mistake to think of political idealism as altruistic—as though it were fueled only by love of humankind. This brand of altruism is more commonly generated by hatred.

3. Those who have responsibility for a country's security have to be alert to signs of disloyalty even though such signs are uncertain. Responsibility of this sort imposes the burden of *balancing* trust in one's associates—a comfort and a necessity—with suspicion. All balances exact costs. As we now know, the cost is the *value* of true positive identifications (he is suspected and he is a spy) and true negatives (he is not suspected and he is not a spy) against the *value* of false positive identifications (he is suspected, but he is not a spy) and false negative identifications (he is judged not to be a spy, but he is).

Given these costs, one can suggest guides for suspicion. These guides are generally the same as those suggested for surveillance of positions of financial trust (Chapter 3). As with all maxims, these too are imperfect:

(a) People in positions of trust who exhibit an appetite for vice should arouse suspicion. Vice includes habitual gambling, habitual intoxication, and sexual promiscuity. Trusted officers who demonstrate their lack of control publicly are doubly suspect. Burgess, for example, was a notorious roisterer and disturber of the peace. His friend, Maclean, was frequently drunk and abusive, the kind of man who broke up parties with his angry loudness. He once displayed his displeasure at his dull company by urinating in front of his guests.

(b) Officials who live beyond their means are also suspect. This practice is often, but not always, associated with a taste for other vices.

(c) Birds of a feather do flock together and suspicion is justifed when the company an officer keeps is hostile to the state that officer is expected to guard. Company includes spouses.

(d) "Verbal droppings" mean something. They should not go unheeded. Offhand comments sometimes speak truer attitudes than those offered under control.

These defenses, and some additional ones, are recommended in response to possible violations of financial trust to be discussed in the next chapter.

3 THEFT BY FRAUD

Abstract • Conceptions of theft depend on conceptions of property. ○ Property excludes. ○ Anarchists therefore seek an end to property as a means of achieving harmony. ○ No moral balance sheets accurately describe costs and benefits of particular modes of holding property. ○ Study of theft proceeds herein within the context of contemporary societies. • Stealing is accomplished by force, fraud, stealth, and their mixture. ○ Some forceful thefts are defined, such as robbery, extortion, intimidation, and mischief. ○ Theft by fraud involves deception. Styles of fraud include violations of trust, embezzlement, false pretenses, forgery, uttering, counterfeiting, personation, arson, con-games, and specific business and political frauds. • Fraud by arson is described. • Styles of con-games are described. • Embezzlement is a particular form of trust violation. Some varied courses leading to embezzlement are described with recommendations for its prevention. • Fraud in business and politics is analyzed as the product of "push and pull." ○ Two classic techniques for committing fraud involve (a) selling what one does not have and (b) robbing Peter to pay Paul or playing the Ponzi. ○ Democratic politics generates deceit and governments play the Ponzi. ○ Parallels are drawn between fraud in politics and swindles in business.

Pierre Joseph Proudhon (1809–1865) taught that "property is theft." His statement sounds profound, but it draws a circle. As we have seen (Chapter 1), the idea of theft *requires* the idea of property. The one notion stands on the other. Without property, there is nothing to steal, and it matters not whether the property is "owned" by individuals, corporations, governments, or "the people."

What Proudhon meant, of course, was that he *disapproved* of private property in particular and of the idea of property in general. In common with others who wish Man to be more cooperative, more altruistic, and less violent, Proudhon saw property as divisive. And it *is* this by definition: a property right is an enforced right to *exclude* others from use of an object or a service.

Enforcement of a right implies force, as the term indicates. It is no wonder, then, that Freud regarded acquisition of property as an *expression* of aggression while Proudhon, Kropotkin, Tolstoy, and other anarchists regarded property as a *stimulus* to aggression. Property probably serves both functions; human beings fight *with* it and they fight *for* it.

Costs and Benefits

We note the connection between systems of property, qualities of theft, and incitement to violence without attempting to strike a balance between the costs and benefits of any particular way of holding property, creating it, and distributing it. It is sufficient here to observe that there are entries on both sides of any moral ledger of social harm and benefit for any system of property.

The point is made because anarchists see no end to misery as long as property separates human beings (Tifft & Sullivan 1980). Other observers see anarchism as inefficient and as subject to the same "iron law of oligarchy" that it condemns. For example, Moore (1972, p. 39) summarizes his study of "the causes of human misery" by holding that, "Mankind can expect to oscillate between the cruelties of law and order and the cruelties of changing it for as long as it leaves the globe fit for human habitation."

Persistence of Property

Some conception of property will persist in the foreseeable future. What communists and anarchists practice is not the abolition of property, but its *transfer* from private to public ownership (Friedmann 1972). But a concept of property persists because it constitutes a major defense against "the tragedy of the commons," that is, against destruction of common resources (Baden 1977, Baden & Stroup 1977, Hardin 1968a). In addition, *private* property constitutes a major defense of the idea of an individual person (Kruse 1953, Lindsay 1932).

All searches for happiness, and health and wealth, involve trade-offs. Recognizing this does not assume that this world is the best of all possible worlds, but it does assume that one person's historical balance sheet will not be another's.

This is said in justification of the study of criminal careers within the context of present societies. It is said because utopian criminologists contend that studying lives within a present context defends a horrible *status quo*. To the contrary, one can observe varied careers in crime, where crime is defined by the laws of a particular state, without assuming its arrangements to be the best conceivable. Moreover, no student of history assumes any social arrangement to be static. The conditions of social life change constantly, but they do not do so in accord with anyone's plan.

With this attitude, we record some of the occasions on which, and some of the means by which, people steal.

DIMENSIONS OF THEFT

Stealing is accomplished by force, fraud, stealth, and their mixture.

Theft by Force

Thievery by force includes the threat of violence as well as its actual use, and "force" includes psychological attacks as well as physical ones.

Robbery is theft effected by violence or its threat. In most jurisdictions, stealing from another person while armed is evidence of robbery, whether or not the weapon is shown and whether or not the armament is imitation or real.

Extortion is a variety of forceful crime usually, but not necessarily, a theft. To extort is to attempt to gain *anything* by threat, accusation, or violence where "anything" is broadly conceived. Thus one can extort business or sexual favors as well as physical property. Moreover, the threat by which the extortion is effected need not be against the person attacked. That is, *Alpha* can extort some action or property from *Beta* by threatening to harm *Beta's* family. Extortion usually carries a lesser penalty than robbery. In Canada, for example, robbers are subject to life imprisonment; extortionists to 14 years imprisonment.

Intimidation, like extortion, may or may not involve theft. It is the crime of compelling another by threat of violence to do anything (s)he has a lawful right not to do, or to refrain from doing anything (s)he has a lawful right to do. As with extortion, the violence may be threatened against intimidated persons, their property, or their families. In most jurisdictions intimidation includes verbal and gestural threats, following persons "in a disorderly manner" on highways, hiding their tools, clothes, or other possessions, "besetting" a person's residence or workplace, and blocking passageways. Whether picket lines constitute intimidation varies with jurisdiction and circumstance.

Mischief is a general term for interference with the use of property. It includes *vandalism,* the willful destruction of others' property.

Theft by Fraud

In Western states most stealing is accomplished by fraud, by stealth, or their mixture. Thievery by fraud involves *deceiving* another person. The duped person may be the victim or the victim's agent.

Theft by stealth is that accomplished by *secrecy*. Some stealing, of course, requires both secrecy and deception.

The crux of the difference between thefts by fraud and by stealth is that frauds are perpetrated on victims who, in varying degrees, are "part of the act" while theft by secrecy is less personal. The difference is that, for example, between a con-game and sneak thievery, between selling "blue sky" and shoplifting, between faking an insurance claim and breaking-and-entering a residence.

Of the three styles of theft—by force, fraud, and stealth—the fraudulent style is the most interesting. It is interesting because it has greater variety. It involves a drama between predators and victims and it frequently combines the injuries of lying and cheating with stealing. In addition, frauds involve more intelligent offenders and larger sums of money than most robberies and burglaries.

A short list of some common thefts by deception shows the variety of fraudulent depredation. This list does not give the full legal definition of each kind of fraud nor does it describe the many techniques employed in effecting each style of deceitful crime.

Violations of trust include thefts by misuse of power of attorney, whether that power is held jointly or singly, and misappropriation of money held "under direction" as to its use by a client. In addition, many states write specific laws concerning "public servants" and their illegal conversion of public property to their own use. Such laws frequently speak of "criminal breaches of trust" beyond those defined by violations of power of attorney.

It is this category of fraud that is commonly referred to as *embezzlement*. Embezzlement is the fraudulent appropriation of others' property left in one's care. It is a crime recognized by the criminal codes of Western countries, but it is not always codified under this title.

Embezzlement is of particular interest to criminologists because it is committed by persons who do not conform to the popular image of the crook. As a consequence, the usual causal explanations advanced for "poor people's thievery" seem inapplicable to "proper person's theft."

Another family of frauds goes by the name of *false pretenses* or *false statements*. False pretenses include representations of matters of fact, either past or present, made by words or other signs, that are known by their makers to be false and that are made with the intent of inducing recipients of the false messages to act upon them.

Western laws try to distinguish harmless exaggeration, as in advertising "puffery," from some degree of misrepresentation that is deemed sufficiently damaging to be criminal. The distinction is difficult at border points and rests on precedents within each jurisdiction.

A sample of false pretenses includes:

1. Obtaining credit by misrepresentation.

2. Obtaining "anything" of value by misrepresenting one's financial condition or the quality of a service or product.

3. Inducing another "to execute, make, accept, endorse, or destroy the whole or part of any valuable security" (Martin & Cartwright 1978, §321).

4. Fraudulently obtaining food and lodging, including having false or pretended baggage, or surreptitiously removing all or part of one's luggage, or absconding, or offering a worthless check or security in payment of one's account.

5. Pretending to practice witchcraft, including sorcery, enchantment, conjuration, telling fortunes, or claiming to have occult powers with which to discover lost valuables.

Laws of this nature are interpreted according to some consensus as to what is and is not "sorcery" and what are the signs of "pretense." Thus astrological prophecies are regularly carried in modern newspapers without prosecution since some consensus regards this mode of fortune-telling as not fraudulently intended.

6. False returns made by public officers.

7. False prospectuses by those offering corporate securities. This includes devices for misrepresenting valuables one is trying to sell, such as "salting" mines.

8. Damaging documents with intent to defraud.

9. Falsifying one's employment record "by any means, including the punching of a time clock" (Martin & Cartwright 1978, §356).

10. Failure to have kept business records when creditors cannot be paid in full.

11. Fraudulent registration or sale of real property or fraudulent concealment of title.

Another category of deceitful theft includes *forgery and related offenses.* Forgery is the *production* of a false document with intent to defraud another through its use. Making a false document includes altering a genuine document by "obliteration, removal, or in any other way" producing a material alteration of its content.

The crime of *uttering a forged document* is that of using it or causing or attempting to cause any other person to use it.

This family of frauds includes producing counterfeit proclamations by governments, sending telegrams under false names with the intent that they be acted upon by another, sending indecent or harassing messages by telephone, radio, or cable, and sending threats by mail, telephone, radio, or cable.

Counterfeiting is part of this family and includes not only the manufacture of fake money, but also the production of false government seals, altering cattle or lumber brands, and damaging official certificates such as election returns and birth, baptism, marriage, divorce, death, and burial documents.

Another variety of fraud is described as *personation*. This is the crime of falsely representing oneself to another person "(a) with intent to gain advantage for oneself or another person, (b) with intent to obtain any property or an interest in any property, or (c) with intent to cause disadvantage to the person whom one personates or another person" (Martin & Cartwright 1978, §361).

This offense includes substituting oneself for another at an examination or having another substitute for oneself. In some jurisdictions, *transvestism* is prosecuted under the charge that one wears clothing of the opposite sex in order to defraud others by such "personation."

These many roads to fraud are but a sample of all the inventions by which thieves of varied commitment to criminal careers take other people's money by deceitful tactics. Some of the more interesting inventions are frauds committed by arson, con-games, embezzlement, and the persistent temptations provided by careers in business and politics.

Arson

Arson is the willful setting of fire to property. It is a crime generated by many motives, only one of which is fraud. Motives include setting fires:

1. For revenge. The urge for vengeance is variously produced, of course, and fire-setting has been observed in children who burn the property of their frustrating parents and in jealous lovers who express their disappointment by torching valuables of their former loves or their rivals.

2. As sabotage in political or industrial disputes. Political fires are set not merely to get one's way in a conflict, but also to express one's hatred of an obstructing group.

3. In satisfaction of a free-floating hostility or as expression of a particular hatred stimulated by religious or racial competition or by envy of someone better off.

4. As a method of murder or in concealment of murder and other crimes.

5. As part of rivalry among leaders of religious or political sects (Canadian Press 1978b).

6. As part of warfare between governments and interest groups. For example, in one American national park, officials believe that 95 percent of their fires are arson, most of which are set to protest restrictions on hunting (Guyon 1980).

7. As a means of sexual gratification. This motive is usually found in cases of chronic fire-setting. The urgency is called *pyromania* and is associated with the satisfaction of both hostile and sexual feelings. The Marquis de Sade gave a description of this perversion in his *The 120 Days of Sodom* (1904).

8. As a fraudulent means of making money.

Arson as an instrument of theft is employed as a defense against bankruptcy but, more commonly, it is a way of defrauding insurance companies.

Arson for profit is currently a "growth crime." The American Insurance Institute, which consists of 400 corporations that write nearly 90 percent of fire insurance policies in the United States, estimates that arson-related crime now costs insurance companies more than $1.5 *billion* annually and that such crime has been increasing at a rate of 20 to 25 percent each year (Murphy 1979). The United States Comptroller General (1978) suggests that the *rate* of American arson doubled between 1971 and 1977 and that arson may be one of America's most costly crimes when one includes in the cost not merely the property lost, but also mortalities and casualties, the loss of tax base and loss of jobs, the increased costs of police, fire, and court services, and the increased price of insurance.

During the 1970s, American arson was given a stimulus by government action. In response to the burning of cities during the race riots of the 1960s, the United States established *Fair Access to Insurance Requirements (FAIR) Plans* in an attempt to guarantee that riot-risk areas would receive insurance. Under these plans, government underwrote losses that private insurance companies were reluctant to assume. A study by the United States General Accounting Office (Comptroller General 1978) concludes that FAIR increased arson by making it profitable.

Arson is a popular form of fraud because it pays. It pays because it is a crime difficult to prove. Prosecutors are therefore reluctant to proceed. They are reluctant also because suspects may sue for punitive damages if cases against them are not proved. Arson pays, too, because the chances of being convicted are about one percent (Comptroller General 1978, p. A-7, Vreeland & Waller 1978). The profitability of arson has promoted gangs that specialize in this lucrative crime and move from city to city.

Gangs and individuals defraud insurance companies in some interesting ways. One technique is to purchase fire insurance from two or more companies and receive full claims for one loss from more than one company. Formation of a national computer file may check this form of fraud (Murphy 1979).

Gangs perpetrate this kind of theft by buying property, listing it under "straw" ownership, insuring it for as much as they comfortably can, having the fake owners mortgage the property to the gang or its agents, burning the property, and claiming the insurance. The United States Comptroller General (1978, p. A-12) describes this typical case:

> A property is purchased at a low price. A few improvements are made, or merely started, to justify an increase in the property's insurable value. The property may be "sold" to a fellow conspirator at an artificially inflated price; the true owner may become the mortgagee. An insurance policy for an amount substantially greater than the market value is often obtained. Shortly after, a fire destroys the property. In one instance, in a Massachusetts FAIR Plan investigation, property purchased for $1,000 was covered by a $25,000 insurance policy. A suspicious fire resulted and the FAIR Plan paid a claim of $16,000.

Steps are being taken to reduce this fraud by:

1. Requiring FAIR Plans to establish property value at the time of insurance underwriting and eliminating the practice of giving property owners any amount of insurance they ask for.

2. Requiring FAIR Plans to investigate the character of owners before insuring them, a practice long used by private insurance companies.

3. Permitting FAIR Plans to use a five-day cancellation notice.

4. Allowing a "broad evidence" rule in deciding the amount to be paid on a claim.

These steps may discourage some arsonists, but the high ratio of return to cost assures continuity of this road to fraud.

Con-Games

In the public image, "cons" are the classic form of fraud. Motion pictures like *The Sting* and other popular presentations have depicted some of the procedures in this style of theft. What amazes workers in criminology and policing is how many "suckers" continue to fall for old frauds despite their publicity. The repeated success of con-games confirms P.T. Barnum's claim that "a sucker is born every minute," but it also attests to the ingenuity of con-artists and their ability to invent variations on old thieving themes. The persistence of successful cons is an indication, too, of the need-to-believe and the perennial willingness, if not eagerness, of people to get something for nothing.

The essence of the con-game is confidence, as the title suggests. The thief steals by exuding confidence and by building the victim's confidence in the thief's story. There are many roads to confidence, of course, and con-artists can travel some routes more easily than others. There is, for example, the "aw-shucks" road on which the artist pretends to be "jes' folks" like the people he or she is conning. And, at the opposite pole, there is the man-of-the-world approach employed by thieves who build confidence by displaying the outer signs of success. All approaches to potential victims operate on the common frailty of assuming that "people like us" are "the right kind of people."

The typical con-game follows a scenario that runs as follows: The *roper* "bird dogs." To "bird dog" is to seek prospects for a sale or a con by almost random procedures. The procedures are not completely haphazard since ropers have some idea where victims may be found for the particular "spiel" (story) they are going to produce. Ropers assume the costume, speech, and attitudes of the *marks* (victims) they seek. Confidence develops through perceived similarity.

The roper's approach to a mark is casual. Introductions are part of some other activity than the business of the con, activities like sports or membership in civic clubs or religious organizations.[1] The fact that the con-man is engaged in that activity is a sign of similarity to the potential mark, and such assumed similarity is its own builder of confidence.

As confidence develops between roper and mark, the *poke* is introduced. The poke is the bait, and it can be any promise of gain, including that of "love," depending on the nature of the game. That is, the lure can vary from the triviality of the "discovered wallet" in the game of *pigeon-drop* to the grander promises of marriage or of gain through insider's investment tips. At this stage, the poke is usually introduced by a confederate of the roper, the *inside man.* The third party's introduction of the bait removes suspicion from the roper and makes it appear that roper and mark are joined in an opportunity to get a quick return at little risk.

Depending on the style of game, the mark may be set up for a big "score" by being allowed to win on minor investments. A little success, a little easy money, expands the appetite.

A con-artist's axiom holds that "you can't con an honest person." A corollary says that "larceny is in everyone's heart" and that the roper is only testing the mark's larcenous threshold. The threshold

---

[1] Some con-men who operate alone specialize in preying on lonely, older women. Church groups are a rich source of such victims.

moves with quantities of promised loot and with styles of obtaining it. The roper, then, is testing the mark to see what "grabs" him or her, to see what the mark wants. Ken Kesey (1964) describes this work in a carnival "grift," but the principle applies generally:

> The secret of being a top-notch conman is being able to know what the mark *wants,* and how to make him think he's getting it. I learned that when I worked a season on a skillo wheel in a carnival. You *fe-e-l* the sucker over with your eyes when he comes up and you say, "Now here's a bird that needs to feel tough." So every time he snaps at you for taking him, you quake in your boots, scared to death, and tell him, "Please, sir, no trouble. The next roll is on the house, sir." So the both of you are getting what you want (p. 74, emphasis his).

In brief, con-artists operate on a tight feed-back loop. They are reading signs of doubt and trust, of hesitancy and greed, until they believe the mark is ready to make the big investment. At this point, the mark is sent for the big money. When (s)he hands it over, the con-artist absconds. The departure is variously arranged and may not be abrupt. It may involve a distracting accident or crime or it may be effected by simple disappearance.

When the mark begins to realize that (s)he has been taken, there may be a tendency "to blow the whistle," that is, to call the police. When this happens, and sometimes before it happens, the roper or a confederate attempts "to cool the mark out." Cooling the mark involves procedures for assuaging the anger and grief at having been victimized. In some con-games, it requires applying *the convincer.* The convincer is not always available, but a preferred application occurs when the con-game has involved the mark in some illegal or immoral activity. Then the *cooler-outer* can persuade the mark that it is cheaper to accept his or her loss than to pursue the criminal.

There are some bold conmen who return to the mark, even after their arrest, to apply a convincer in an effort to initiate a second round of investment. Lonely ladies, and some lonely men, are suckers for this repeated persuasion.

The con-artist's weapon is words. He creates images with them, and promises a better life. The famous con-man Yellow Kid Weil once justified himself to the novelist Saul Bellow by saying, "How was I to live? My power lay in words. In words I become a commander." (cited by Tanner 1965, p. 60).

A good con-man lies so convincingly he may come to believe his own lies. Only a hazy boundary separates brazen swindling from gulling a customer, a voter, or a religious devotee (Leff 1976).

Career Pleasures

If one finds it necessary to ask why con-artists engage in their work, the best answer is that they enjoy it. They enjoy the income gained in relative safety and with independence from a boss. They take pride in their workmanship and gain reputations as their skills improve and become known to other swindlers. They are proud of their acting ability and their cleverness in "reading" the mark.

They enjoy the errant life, a life of wandering and irresponsibility. Kesey (1964, p. 84) describes this pleasure as, "No wife wanting new linoleum. No relatives pulling at him with watery old eyes. No one to *care* about, which is what makes him free enough to be a good con man" (emphasis his). One such adventurer put the joy of his work this way, "I've eaten in the best restaurants, traveled in the best company, and left a million unmade beds."

Last, just as most people find gambling fun because of the risk and the promise, so conning is fun for the artist in fraud.

Prescription

On the record, no con-artist has been cured by preachment or any known therapy. And, in opposition to some theories of crime-production that see "limited opportunities" as the generator of criminal careers, the con-man prefers the illegitimate opportunities he exploits to the legitimate ones he knows.

The most reliable cure of the con-artist is age. Debilities of age reduce nerve and skill and make perpetual mobility less fun.

Embezzlement

A con-artist differs from an embezzler in accepting theft as his vocation. By contrast, an embezzler takes a legitimate job *without* the intention, at the time, of using it as a medium of larceny. If a thief does assume a position of trust in order to violate it, (s)he is better regarded as a variety of con-artist.

The distinction is important for explanation and protection. Embezzlers appear to be "straight" persons prior to their arrest. They are usually middle- or upper-class individuals who do not conform to the background or the image of "the textbook crook." They therefore challenge some criminological theories about crime causation.

A Map of One Road

Until recently, the most popular explanation of embezzlement was that advanced by Donald R. Cressey in his study, *Other People's*

Money (1953, 2nd edition 1971). Cressey attempted to employ "the limited case method" or method of "analytic induction" (Znaniecki 1934) in understanding how well-advantaged persons could be converted to thieves. The central proposition of the method of analytic induction is that explanation of conduct proceeds most fruitfully through description of events in such a way that certain personal traits, or antecedent conditions, are *always* present when the explanandum (thing to be explained) occurs and *never* present in its absence. In short, this is a search for a uniform course to embezzlement. If the search succeeds, it challenges our theme of "many roads."

Cressey's proposed single course to a violation of financial trust includes four steps. These four kinds of event are alleged to occur *without exception* as a lawful person is caused to steal. They are:

1. That the embezzler-to-be is in a position of financial trust and that the position was initially accepted without the intention of using it to steal.

2. That the trusted person develops what Cressey calls a "non-shareable problem." Definition of such a "problem" is vague and the illustrations provided run a gamut of difficulties. However, the "problem" is deemed to be soluble in money and, most important for Cressey's hypothesis, it is *not shared.* Presumably, a difficulty that is discussed with others will not lead to this crime.

3. That the once-honest person en route to becoming a thief has technical skills for stealing. This is a minor step in the causal chain since any person in a position of financial responsibility learns how to violate it.

4. That the embezzler acquires a thought-process, a rationalization, that justifies stealing. The usual rationalization calls the theft "borrowing," but whatever it is called, the justification is, for Cressey, the *motive.*

In support of his hypothesis, Cressey reports that interviews with 133 imprisoned embezzlers in three of the United States and a reading of some 200 cases in his mentor's (E.H. Sutherland's) files revealed no exceptions to a crime-binding process as described in the four steps above.

Criticism

The method of analytic induction has been criticized in general (Robinson 1951, Turner 1953) and in its particular applications to criminology (Ausubel 1958, Clinard 1954, Hagan 1971, Schuessler 1954). However, Cressey's explanation of embezzlement endured because, for many years, no competing hypothesis was available and because its explanatory theme is that of *symbolic interactionism,* the most popular interpretation of social psychology among sociologists. Nevertheless, the attempted description of a single road to embezzlement has many faults:

1. The method of analytic induction conceives the causes of this crime only after the criminal act and never before the fact. It produces plausible stories after the offender is apprehended, but it provides no premonitory cues. It is a way of interpreting traces, but not of reading portents.

2. This procedure for understanding embezzlement adds nothing to predictive power because the search for universals that, without exception, produce a particular event can function only by describing alleged causes in vague terms. This vagueness assures plausibility and it provides a defense against falsification.

For example, in Cressey's thesis, the idea of a "problem" is presented in such general terms that, after the fact of having committed a crime, all persons can be deemed to have had some "problem."[2] Everyone has "problems," if difficulties and desires are described in general terms. With such a broad and non-defining "definition," the differentiae that mark criminal and non-criminal courses are not specified.

3. Cressey's explanatory schema, that of symbolic interactionism, assumes that certain mental events, variously called beliefs, attitudes, and definitions of the situation, cause conduct. This school of social psychology attributes decision to thought and conduct to its justification. It accepts words as valid indicators of motives and rationalizations as crucial elements in a causal chain.

This description of the generation of conduct is congenial, but it is not very useful. It lacks explanatory power because it is difficult, if not impossible, to observe a person's attitude or definition of the situation separately from the acts these mental processes are supposed to cause. *Belief* is known by what a person says *and* does. An utterance that is not accompanied by some appropriate doing is considered to be mere verbalization, not "belief."

Given the difficulties of ascertaining the conditions under which one's words accurately describe one's motives, it is impossible to assign differential causal force to particular utterances. Justifications can

---

[2] Once a person has been arrested and a search initiated for "what is wrong with him/her," some psychologist or psychiatrist can find "something wrong" with anyone. The "something wrong" may have nothing to do with causing the crime, however.

be rationalizations offered after one has been caught. They may or may not have been motives in operation as the crime is produced.

4. A Canadian test of Cressey's hypothesis assessed six important cases of embezzlement during the 1960s and early 1970s (Nettler 1974). This study involved interviews with convicted embezzlers and included psychometric testing of three of the offenders. In only one of the six cases could Cressey's singular course to a crime be discerned. The study concludes that:

> Our thieves stole from a variety of motives, in a variety of circumstances, and out of different backgrounds. Occupationally and sexually they consist of two male attorneys, one female bookkeeper, one female bank cashier, one male social worker, and one male investment counsellor. In our assessment the one embezzler who conforms to Cressey's model was an attorney whose charm, confidence, and enterprise involved friends in a wide stream of under-capitalized investments. Out of concern for his own name and his friends' fortunes, money left in trust was "borrowed" until it was beyond recovery and the theft was discovered.
>
> The five other embezzlers investigated did not steal out of any similar set of circumstances. With one possible exception, none of the remaining offenders initiated his or her series of thefts because of being "in a crack," to use Cressey's phrase. The possible exception that might be described as a person "in a bind" was a man who had been renting a farm and its buildings and improving the property. When the farm was to be sold and our subject to be evicted, he converted funds left in his trust so that he could purchase the estate. In this case, however, the "problem," how to keep the beloved land, was *not* unshared. It was fully and repetitively discussed with the embezzler's wife (p. 74).

Other Roads

The Canadian study found other routes to embezzlement besides that characterized by an unshared financial difficulty leading to theft justified as "temporary borrowing." Two of these routes have long been observed by detectives and auditors.

The detective's explanation has been nicknamed the hypothesis of the "Three B's"—babes, booze, and bets. Confronted with embezzlement, detectives tend to assume that what turns a straight man, or woman, crooked is some variable combination of sex, the alcoholic "sweet life," and gambling. Their advice to partners and employers is always to be alert to signs of vice and to indications that a trusted person is living beyond his or her means. Detectives are not interested in rationalizations.

The auditor's hypothesis agrees with that of detectives, but it goes further. Auditors assume that theft is generated by some meeting of *desire* and *opportunity*. Vice is only one generator of desire, and the temptation to take money that is readily available is deemed to be a timeless possibility for all of us.

Intensity of desire and conception of opportunity are personality variables. The balance between desire and opportunity moves. Temptation to steal fluctuates with individual temperament and situation. The Canadian assessment points out that:

> In two [of the cases] the opportunities were so open for so long that it would have required strong defenses or weak desires to resist enjoying other people's money. For example, a social worker in charge of a welfare agency resisted for seven years stealing the inadequately guarded funds entrusted to him. Only after these years of handling easy money did he succumb to the pleasures of acquiring some $25,000. annually in "welfare payments" made to non-existent clients. These benefits accrued for eight years before his arrest. The thefts were *not* engaged to meet a secret financial difficulty. They did, of course, *produce* an unshareable financial embarrassment. In this case, money was stolen because it was, like Everest, there (Nettler 1974, p. 75, emphasis his).

Similarly, Maxwell (1972, 1973) reports one of the largest solo embezzlements in North American history. It confirms the auditor's hypothesis. This easy theft of at least $4.7 *million* by a small-town banker cannot be explained by the strain of an "unshared problem." It is better explained by the conjunction of desire and opportunity.

Desire sometimes overwhelms opportunity, and opportunity sometimes creates desire. For example, one of the Canadian cases occurred because the "male" in a lesbian liaison wished to please her loved one. Getting the money to do this required invention of an elaborate scheme for milking the bank in which the offender worked.

The implication of this research is that all people may be expected to steal if opportunity is repeatedly presented, where "opportunity" is interpreted as a chance to gain with little risk of loss. This assumption leads to advice different from that which follows from Cressey's hypothesis.[3]

---

[3] A test of competing theories is what they differentially predict. In the present case, one would like to test which sets of recommendations, made in congruence with their respective interpretations of action, lead to the greater proportion of successful forecasts. Such a controlled, prospective test of the different explanations of embezzlement has not been made. However, retrospective tests—that is, those based on experience—lend more credence to auditors' and detectives' hypotheses than to Cressey's.

Competing Advice

Consistent with his hypothesis, Cressey (1964, pp. 25–26) offers two pieces of advice to consumers of his explanation of embezzlement:

1. That companies start programs designed to reduce those "unshared problems" believed to create temptation to violate an employer's trust.

2. That companies institute "education programs emphasizing the nature of the verbalizations commonly used by trust violators." "We must," Cressey advises, "make it increasingly difficult for trusted employees . . . to think of themselves as "borrowers' rather than as 'thieves' when they take the boss's money."

Other Advice

The soundness of this advice rests on the clarity and power of the causes nominated by Cressey. These causes, selected by a symbolic interactionist interpretation of conduct, are neither clear nor powerful, and the advice that follows from this explanation is poor.

By contrast, prescriptions that follow from detectives' and auditors' explanations urge reduction of opportunities to steal and alertness to signs of appetites that exceed financial means. These prescriptions assume that vice creates financial need and lowers the threshold of temptation. Some specific recommendations for employers and partners are these:

1. Be reluctant to employ persons with records of frequent job changes, vice, and high indebtedness.

2. After hiring, be suspicious of "high living."

In substantiation of these two recommendations, Redden (1939) compared the careers of 2,454 embezzlers with those of 7,756 lawful persons in similar positions on 22 items used as screening devices by bonding companies. Statistical analysis of scores on these items combined them in clusters of information from which experience tables were constructed. These tables were then cross-validated on 500 embezzlers and 500 lawful control subjects and shown to discriminate between them.

Redden found people at risk of becoming embezzlers to have had higher indebtedness, less property, more job changes, and lower monthly incomes than their lawful counterparts. She also found that "outside" employees and those working on commission had nearly double their quota of embezzlers. Others who were found to be at risk of embezzlement were men, married persons, blacks, and foreign-born individuals.

3. Be suspicious of employees who refuse promotion.

One motive for wishing to remain in a job niche is that the employee has a "good scam" working.

4. Require all employees to take an annual vacation. During the holidays of cashiers or bookkeepers, statements should be sent to customers.

5. Never allow one person to handle all phases of a financial transaction.

Securities and other negotiable valuables should be under the control of two or more officers. Counter-signatures should be required on all checks over an established sum. Checks in payment of bills should be mailed by someone other than the person who orders payment and someone other than the person who prepares the check. The person who computes payroll should *not* be the person who distributes it.

6. Take inventory frequently, as is feasible, and have the inventory counted by someone other than the person in charge of stock.

These prescriptions are costly. Their cost has to be assessed by each employer or partner against the cost of a possible loss. Computerization of financial records increases the size (cost) of possible loss. "Computer jockeys" now have many opportunities to steal large amounts of money. Their technical expertise and their solo work lower the threshold of temptation and make their discovery more difficult. The "white collar" status of such embezzlers and the embarrassment of the employers from whom they steal reduce risk of prosecution. Restitution is sought instead of prosecution. And when such offenders are convicted, their penalties tend to be light given the amounts they have stolen. The first line of defense against this and other styles of embezzlement is in multiple auditing checks (Bequai 1978, Krauss & MacGahan 1979).

Recent Examples

Within a span of three months in 1981, three American banks discovered that trusted officers had stolen large sums. The Beverly Hills branch of the Wells Fargo Bank lost a reported 21.3 million dollars, the Chase Manhattan Bank of New York City was out some 20 million dollars, and Houston's Allied Bank of Texas lost about 17 million dollars (*Economist* 1981, Lancaster & Hill 1981, *Time* 1981).

In each case senior executives have been accused of the embezzlement and in each case there was violation of one or more of our six prescriptions. All these frauds worked for a while because one person was allowed unchecked control over financial transactions. In addition, the Wells Fargo theft was facilitated by the accused banker's weekly visits to the office computer, whether or not he was officially on holiday. In the Houston case, the vice-president accused of looting the Allied Bank lived far better than his salary would allow. He owned a cattle-breeding business spread over six states and was a habitué of the Houston nightclub circuit where he was noted for his lavish tips to topless dancers. It was assumed that he had a silent partner financing his business ventures and no questions were asked.

Flamboyant living by those who handle other people's money does not prove guilt, but it is a cue that deserves attention.

Fraud in Business and Politics

The simplest explanation of lying, cheating, and stealing notes the short-term advantage to the deceitful, where "advantage" is, of course, a function of what the individual wants and where the causes of differences in wants are sought among all the factors discussed in Volume One.

Economists find advantage at the junction of appetite and opportunity. They ignore differences in individual desire because, as Rubin (1980, pp. 13–14) puts it, "we have absolutely no theory of changes in tastes . . . and therefore an explanation that relies on tastes is tautological—that is, such an explanation can explain anything and therefore is not useful for scientific purposes." This means that economists predict that action moves with rewards and costs.

This assumption may be good enough for drawing crude causal diagrams of the roads to crime. But, in the study of individual careers, it omits the significant personal variables of preference for risk, vocational interest, resistance to temptation, and desire for wealth and power. Contrary to Rubin, one need not have a theory of *change* of tastes in order to observe *variation* in tastes that are correlated with particular kinds of conduct. We are reminded that, as Chapter 6, Volume One, showed, reward and punishment cannot be abstractly defined but are individually appreciated.

This is said because not all persons in similar situations behave the same way. And when one looks at fraud in business and politics, it is apparent that, while the economist's general description of the conditions of theft is valid, it omits much when it omits individual preferences for ways of doing business and styles in politics.

Another obscurity persists in the economist's simple explanation of crime. This explanation does not account for *levels* of criminal activity. It does not explain why almost everyone is not a thief of greater caliber. For research indicates that the average thief in the United

States has "about a two percent chance of being arrested, prosecuted, and convicted for any given offense of this kind" (Jones 1979, p. 37). This estimate probably holds also for Canada and Great Britain.

Moreover, Jones (1979, p. 38) adds, "the greater the volume of crime in which each offender participates, the greater the profits from crime. Not only will the large-volume criminal offender *gross* more rewards from crime, he will *net* more rewards in terms of his after-taxes profits. . . ." (emphasis his). Clearly, even a small risk of apprehension has different value for different individuals.

A laboratory experiment demonstrates this fact. Carroll (1978) tested considerations that affect decisions to commit a crime. He had juvenile and adult males, offenders and non-offenders, rank three opportunities to steal on four dimensions:

1. the probability that the crime would be successful;
2. the amount of money to be obtained if one were successful;
3. the probability of being caught; and
4. the severity of the penalty if one were caught.

In the laboratory at least, the decision to commit a crime is most significantly determined by the amount of money to be gained. Severity of penalty, probability of success, and probability of capture were ranked in that order, but with considerable less importance than the amount of money to be taken. What is significant for present purposes is that *individuals differ* in their use of these rewards and costs of crime and that offenders in Carroll's sample rated all criminal opportunities as more desirable than did non-offenders. Carroll concludes that "making crime less profitable in comparison to noncrime opportunities may have stronger effects on crime rates than increasing the likelihood and severity of punishment" (p. 1512).

Push and Pull

With the qualification that individuals make a difference, one can accept the general economic rule that conceived advantage motivates fraud. There are two sides to the motivation: the attraction of wealth and power and the need to defend what one has. Metaphorically, these are occasions that pull or push one toward fraud.

Conception of advantage in business and politics can be generated, on the one hand, by the "pull" of money and power. On the other hand, one can be "pushed" toward fraud by "being in a bind" or "getting in a crack." These occasions are sometimes described as "pressures" that make fraud seem rational.

Some of these opportunities and pressures are briefly described.

MONEY MOTIVATES

The object of business and industry in capitalist countries is to make money. Money is a wonderful stimulant but, like all stimulants, it exacts a cost. One price paid for energizing by capital acquisition and investment is the temptation to get more by cheating.

Contrary to theories of criminogenesis that see theft generated only by "need" or by "restricted opportunity," some big frauds are produced simply by the desire to be richer than one is. Whatever a person presently feels about "how much would be enough," once one has more it seems like less. Appetites expand with their feeding.

This is the history, and explanation, of the grandest business fraud of this century: The Equity Funding Corporation scandal, known as "Wall Street's Watergate." The scandal was fueled by inflation which, in turn, is generated by government policies.

Inflation makes conservative savings useless. Money melts as it is kept in savings accounts or in securities with a constant pay-off. This fact stimulates ideas for getting ahead of the game. One such idea is that of *leverage*. Leverage is the practice of borrowing money on assets one owns in the expectation that the borrowed funds can be used to make more money than the cost of the interest on the loan. It is the idea of using one's money twice.

This idea was incorporated as a "concept" in the sale of life insurance by a few aggressive salesmen. Gordon McCormick may have invented the "concept" in the 1950s, although he denies it and says the invention was just "an idea whose time had come." In the life insurance business, leverage is gained by selling "the combination," an investment in mutual funds, the equity in which is then used as collateral for a loan with which to buy life insurance. A prospectus of Equity Funding outlines the steps:

> INVEST . . . First, you invest in shares of a mutual fund;
>
> INSURE . . . Second, you select a life insurance program;
>
> BORROW . . . Third, you borrow against your mutual fund shares to pay each annual insurance program;
>
> REPAY LOAN . . . Fourth, at the end of ten years you pay the principal and interest on the premium loan, either in cash, in part from any insurance cash values, or by redeeming shares;
>
> RESULT . . . Any appreciation from your investment in excess of the amount owed is your profit (cited by Dirks & Gross 1974, pp. 19–20).

In a complicated chain of events, McCormick met four other men eager for money and thus began the Equity Funding Corporation. It is normal for partners to squabble and, after one such dispute, McCormick sold his interest in the company that was to become the darling of Wall Street.

The four associates who spawned Equity Funding were united by one impulse: greed. Otherwise, as Dirks and Gross (1974, p. 12) describe them, "They were as different as diamonds, one the Irish heir to a Jewish department store, the second a gambling lush, the third a sportsman, the fourth a brooding ex-butcher."

Michael Riordan was a big, good-looking extrovert. His father was vice-president of Abraham & Strauss, a department store chain. Riordan knew no poverty, but he had the financial zeal of a go-getting salesman. He loved women, booze, and bets. His slogan was, "Every night is opening night." His theme song was "The Impossible Dream." His goal was to get to California and make a hundred million dollars. He almost did it, but he was killed at age 41 by a mudslide that buried him in his Mandeville Canyon home.

Raymond Platt was a second initiator. He too was a powerful salesman and a hard drinker. Success with Equity Funding exacerbated the drinking and gambling and led to bar brawls and bad checks. Platt promised his partners that he would reform, but character is firmer than promise and, in 1962, Platt was fired as an officer of the company. A few months after his removal, he had a barroom fight with Riordan. Platt followed this with a lawsuit claiming that he had been improperly excluded from Equity Funding and demanding 20 percent of company assets and profits. A heart attack knocked him off a barstool and he was dead at age 38. His widow pursued his lawsuit without success.

Eugene Cuthbertson was the third man to join in formation of Equity Funding. He was an engineering graduate who moved in different social circles from Riordan and Platt. His wife was a socialite and his association with the brash salesmen was limited. In 1965, after disputes with his partners, Cuthbertson sold his shares in Equity Funding for a net gain of $870,000.

The fourth man in the drama was the one to take over Equity Funding and expand it into fraud—Stanley Goldblum. In contrast to Platt and Riordan, Goldblum was judged to be brilliant, but not a salesman. He was however, a commander. Dirks and Gross (1974, pp. 34–35) describe him:

> Physically, he was awesome. He measured six feet two inches, but such was his muscular bulk that colleagues assured you he was six four. He looked like an ex-boxer or -wrestler. His small, almond-shaped eyes gave his heavy face a faint, incongruous Mongolian caste. He made people wonder if he was comfortable doing what he did. But his manner left no

doubts that, comfortable or not, he was in command. He broadcast
power. He wanted, and took, control of all proceedings. He would slice
into discussions. He was impatient, assertive, steely, crisp.

Eight years after four men seized control of a tiny insurance company, Goldblum was alone—the chief executive of a company with
assets of $497 million, with revenues for 1971 of $131 million and net
earnings for that year of $19 million.

Goldblum built Equity Funding in two legal ways: by selling policies through "the combination" and by presenting such an image of
success that the price of Equity Funding shares escalated. By 1970
Goldblum was worth about $30 million. He received a salary of
$100,000 a year plus $150,000 to $200,000 in stock bonuses each year.
He lived in a Beverly Hills mansion and enjoyed a yacht, dirt bikes,
and exotic automobiles. He built a $100,000 gym adjoining his house
where he "pushed iron." When asked why he lifted weights, he re-
plied, "For size." This theme, getting bigger, characterized his business goal as it did his physical goal.

Getting bigger involved purchases of other companies and spin-
offs. Equity Funding managed three subsidiary insurance companies
and three mutual funds. It owned a petroleum exploration company,
a cattle-breeding operation, a bank, and a savings and loan association. However, fraud began before great size was reached and it was
one of the methods employed to get bigger. Fraud involved two related techniques for stealing. These schemes constitute classic styles
of fraud: selling something one does not have and robbing Peter to
pay Paul.

Two Classic Techniques

Given the nature of much investment, it is possible to sell what
one does not have. Numbers on accountants' books need bear no relation to anything of value.

In this manner, some expensive frauds have recently involved sale
of $3.2 million worth of nonexistent cattle (Penn 1973), $6 million
worth of anhydrous ammonia stored in empty tanks (*Time* 1962), $30
million worth of nonexistent petroleum (*Wall Street Journal* 1973),
$219 million worth of imaginary vegetable oil (*Time* 1965), $58 million worth of fake business assets (Williams 1967), and more than
$120 million worth of nonexistent petroleum and real estate
(McClintick 1977).

Equity Funding sold life insurance policies to "re-insurers" written
on nonexistent persons. It prepared applications for insurance writ-

ten in the name of imaginary people. It then "sold" policies to these ghosts and re-sold the fake documents to re-insurers. It is normal for insurance companies to sell part of their risks to other companies so that no one claim can hurt an insurer. But Equity Funding had its "Department 99" pumping out forged documents. When the nonexistent persons "died," Equity Funding collected from re-insurers.

The Ponzi

A cousin of the scheme to sell numbers representing nothing is the con named after one of its more successful practitioners, Charles Ponzi. Just after World War I, Ponzi invented a form of arbitrage with which to fleece investors. *Arbitrage* is the legitimate work of simultaneously buying and selling securities or monies of different countries in order to profit from quickly changing differences in exchange rates.

Ponzi devised a form of arbitrage with international money orders and postal certificates (Dunn 1975). Ponzi offered to pay investors 50 percent interest every 45 days. He did this partly out of legitimate dealing in arbitrage, but mostly, and increasingly, by paying old investors with new investors' money. The scheme is like that of the chain letter or "pyramid." It works as long as cash flow exceeds the pay-out. The secret of the con is to abscond when one is ahead; the temptation of the con for the artist is to get a little more.

Governments play the Ponzi, as we shall see, and Equity Funding worked this fraud by buying successful companies with which to shore up the mother firm whose assets were largely fictitious.

The Ponzi works on the same kind of optimism that stimulates embezzlement: "Just a little more, and a little time, and then we'll be in the clear." But "accidents" happen. There is a "run" and demand for payment exceeds cash on hand, or someone "blows the whistle."

In the Equity Funding case both accidents occurred. Interestingly, one of the securities analysts who "blew the whistle," Raymond Dirks, was himself sued by Equity Funding stockholders for the losses they incurred upon revelation of company fraud. However, in 1973, a federal grand jury indicted 22 men, including Goldblum and two members of an accounting firm, on 105 criminal counts. The charges included securities fraud, mail fraud, bank fraud, interstate transportation of counterfeit securities, electronic eavesdropping, and filing false documents with the Securities and Exchange Commission. The total amount stolen is difficult to estimate, but it probably exceeds $100 million (Dirks & Gross 1974, pp. 237–238).

Implication

What is of interest to students of criminal careers is that these crimes were not produced by poverty, need, or pressure. They were invented for the pleasures of wealth.

It is also of interest that many employees remained silent although they were aware of the work in forgery. Dirks and Gross (1974, p. 239) think that as many as 100 employees must have known of their company's illegal activities although only about 20 men were deeply involved in the dirty work. However, only a few persons reported their suspicions to authorities. The motives for silence were common ones: The wish to keep one's job, reluctance to "get involved," and, finally, approval of the con as a means of "making it."

These big thieves were dishonest crooks. They did not regard their frauds as thefts. Ironically, Stanley Goldblum was for a while chairman of the "business conduct" committee of the Los Angeles branch of the National Association of Securities Dealers where he was harsh on transgressors of business ethics.

This story describes a "pull" toward fraud. Another variety of "dishonest fraud" is that committed under the "push" of business and politics.

Rational Deceit

Demands for production in factory, field, board room, school room, and political arena stimulate fraud when the subjectively appreciated value of an objective exceeds the subjectively appreciated guilt or shame[4] induced by the deceit. Ends *do* justify means—not in some abstract, philosophical realm, but in the everyday world of action. Ends are *used* to justify means.

Thus, in the factory, production quotas and quality control standards encourage faking when they exceed possibility or some norm of work. For example, Vandivier (1972) describes how the need to produce fighter aircraft on a tight schedule produced shortcuts in quality control. Competition for the work led to underestimation of the time required to complete it which, in turn, led to "pressure" on supervisors to pass defective equipment as sound.

---

[4] In psychological terms, guilt refers to one's sense of wrong-doing—whether or not one is caught. Shame refers to embarrassment at having been caught.

Guilt may be evoked by real or imagined wrong-doing. Shame is evoked by looking in a public mirror that one acknowledges reflects truly.

This example is a model of the generation of cheating in factory and field. Unrealistic objectives, set by superiors or by the structure of the work, produce fraud when workers cannot opt out.

In similar fashion, corporation executives invent deceptive schemes when competition threatens profit. The so-called "incredible electrical conspiracy" (Smith 1961) is an example of the rationality of cheating. Some of the world's largest manufacturers of electrical equipment colluded to "rig" bids and thus divide more securely and economically a market for their products valued at about $2 billion a year. In this conspiracy, 45 executives of 29 corporations were indicted for violating the Sherman Antitrust Act.

Principals in this crime regarded the objective of "rational business cooperation" as more valuable than the objectives of the antitrust legislation. Antitrust laws claim legitimacy as "socially protective." However, the concept of "social harm" to which such laws appeal is *not* the same as that reflected in the traditional crimes *mala in se.* There is running debate, therefore, whether such legislation is wrong or the conspiracy to violate it criminal (Thurow 1980). Japan, for example, allows collaboration between businesses that is prohibited in the United States (Holden 1980, Patrick & Rosovsky 1976).

However, there is less dispute about other forms of corporate crime such as fraud and bribery, although it needs to be noted that bribery is condemned in Nordic and North American countries while it is a normal accompaniment of business in Latin and Middle Eastern countries. The extent of "corporate corruption" in the United States is indicated by Irwin Ross's (1980) study of 1,043 major American firms during the 1970s. Ross counted convictions and consent decrees (in which companies neither admit nor deny past crimes but agree not to commit them in the future) for five classes of offense: bribery, tax evasion, fraud, illegal political contributions, and criminal antitrust violations such as price-fixing and bid-rigging. Ross finds that:

> [One hundred and seventeen] or 11 percent [of the companies studied] have been involved in at least one major delinquency [during the 1970s]. Some companies have been multiple offenders. In all, 188 citations are listed covering 163 separate offenses. ... This roll call of wrongdoing is limited to domestic cases; the list would have been longer had it included foreign bribes and kickbacks (p. 57).

Ross's tally would also have been larger had he been able to count the crimes of small business proprietors that include such varieties of theft as "skimming" profits and short-weighting packages.

What is significant for criminologists is that actors under varieties of "pressures" in factory, field, and office justify their violations by claiming to be honorable persons, by referring to their predicaments, and, sometimes, by claiming rules of the game to be unfair. One executive put it this way:

> We're not vicious enemies in this industry, but rather people in similar binds. I've always thought of myself as an honorable citizen. We didn't do these things for our own behalf [but] for the betterment of the company (Sonnenfeld & Lawrence 1978, p. 148).

Similar justifications are voiced by fraudulent actors in politics.

Democracy and Deceit

Lying is a hazard of political work. This has long been recognized and many advisors have recommended deceit as a tactic in inter-tribal strife (Guicciardini 1965, Machiavelli 1513). But, of more moment to us is the way in which democratic politics in heterogeneous societies promotes fraud.

Propaganda as Part-Time Fraud

Political fraud consists only in part of campaign "puffery" and the use of vague words and grand promises to elicit votes. Propaganda may, or may not, be fraudulent.

Propaganda is properly understood to be the use of symbols to move people to act in a desired way. The symbols can be words, costumes, gestures, and sounds. Their function is to create an image, rather than a comprehensible proposition, and to create such an image of heroes, villains, and good objectives that consumers of the symbols will be moved in the "right" direction. These symbols may create accurate images or false ones. There is nothing in the origin of the idea of propaganda that says it must be false.[5] In fact, successful propagandists prefer truth to lies—if the truth is on their side (Ellul 1965, p. 53).

Propaganda in political campaigns is best conceived, then, as part-time fraud. It consists of stories that are partly true, partly false, and sometimes just obscure. Larger frauds are induced by the push to play Ponzi generated by the need to "buy" votes.

---

[5] Modern use of the word, "propaganda" derives from "The Congress for the Propagation of the Faith" established by Pope Gregory XV in 1622.

Governmental Ponzi

The task of a politician in a heterogeneous democracy is to attain and maintain power by getting the support of voters who are increasingly organized as interest groups. Interest groups form around issues, and these can be moral preferences or economic demands. With growth of central governments and popularization of the assumption that governments exist to satisfy "needs," it is easy to learn that one way to get is to demand—as a price of one's vote. Thus, ethnicity has become a lively issue in societies that used to preach individual regard because organizing as a "minority" pays off (Glazer & Moynihan 1975).

It is now widely assumed that governments exist to give things to people. This assumption confirms Voltaire's (1764) definition, that "the art of government consists in taking as much money as possible from one class of citizens to give to the other." Voltaire came to believe this as he saw France slide toward the bankruptcy that produced its great revolution. After the revolution, the French economist Frédéric Bastiat (1801–1850) repeated Voltaire's definition more forcefully: "The state," he said, "is that great engine by which everyone seeks to live at the expense of everyone else."

Modern governments play Ponzi by spending more than they have. They finance the deficit by borrowing. The rational justification for borrowing is that more can be earned with this leverage than without it and that increased future earnings will pay principal and interest on the debt and leave a surplus. This kind of optimism is sometimes justified, as in situations where real economic growth is possible. However, this optimism is similar to that which, we've seen, motivates some embezzlers.

Borrowing is accomplished, of course, by promising. Debtors promise to return principal to investors plus interest. But, lacking real economic growth, governments then borrow yet more to pay back what was originally borrowed. They are on a deceitful course and one road to fraud.

In the modern world two kinds of government are vulnerable to deficit spending: (a) socialist dictatorships concerned to expropriate property and redistribute it without attention to the conditions under which wealth is produced and (b) democracies. In democracies, politicians compete for votes. In the competition, those who reduce taxes and increase expenditures tend to gain voters' approval. Conversely, those who attempt to increase taxes and reduce expenditures tend to lose support. This means that economic decisions are made for political reasons. Such decisions make for short-term political success and long-term economic failure. The American and British records can be read in works by Buchanan et al. (1978), Buchanan and Wagner (1977), Crain and Ekelund (1978), Drucker (1980), Tufte (1978), and Wagner and Tollison (1980).

Unless wealth is generated by economic growth stimulated by the borrowing, governments find themselves "in a bind." One way out of their difficulty is to print money and devalue currency. Creditors are then paid back with cheaper money. Inflation consumes the substance of a government's promise to its investors. For example, if a state sells its bonds with a promise to return, say, six percent to investors, and if its inflation runs at double that rate, the government is involved in a cheat. People begin to notice the trick and some take action. Thus, a Gray Panther attorney recently complained to the U.S. Federal Trade Commission that government advertisements for its savings bonds were misleading. They claimed to be a hedge against inflation when they were yielding a return five points less than the inflation rate. The advertisement was revised (*Wall Street Journal* 1980d).

Meanwhile, incomes that grow with inflation push higher proportions of taxpayers into higher tax brackets and allow governments some "breathing space" in their Ponzi's. This inflationary shove increases returns to treasuries without the unpopular necessity of legislating higher taxes and without an increase of wealth—the economic base—from which the tax is taken.

Some people may benefit from gradual inflation—home owners, for example, legislators, and civil servants whose salaries are indexed to inflation but not to production. However, unless one can keep the "pyramid" going with fresh infusions of wealth,[6] a day of reckoning arrives when people get wise to the game, lose confidence in the government's ability to repay their loans, and refuse to invest further. Wealth flees abroad and business capitalization declines.

The German disaster of the 1920s, the Chinese debacle of the 1930s, and Hungary's troubles in the 1940s are prime examples of economies damaged by government-induced inflation. In Germany, money literally became worthless. When government stopped printing currency and issued a gold mark, the exchange ratio was *one trillion* paper marks for one gold mark. In China, prices increased in a decade by 151.73×10^{12} and in Hungary, in little more than one year,

---

[6] In healthy economies, money is one measure of wealth—that is, of something of value in exchange or in use. In weak economies, money is paper with an uncertain and varying relation to ability to command wealth or produce it (Groseclose 1967, Jastram 1977, Lehrman 1980).

prices jumped by 399.62 x 10^{27} (Chou 1963, Davidson 1980, pp. 77–78). The economies of Allende's Chile, of Argentina, Brazil, Uruguay, Italy, Jamaica, and Great Britain provide more recent cases of state-induced inflation eroding a standard of living.

During the inflationary process, governmental Ponzi may be legal without being honest. It might be called "stealing without thieving." However, playing Ponzi puts one on the slippery slope toward fraud. As cash flow slows, as borrowing becomes more difficult, as money is divorced from wealth, politicians and their bureaucrats are pushed toward misrepresenting government finances. Accounting becomes shady. Fraud is committed. New York City, which in 1969 debated becoming the 51st state, illustrates how governments go broke and how the course toward bankruptcy generates deceit.

Good Intentions and Cooked Books

The investigative reporter Ken Auletta (1975a, 1975b, 1979) believes that government officials and bankers in New York City committed "the biggest securities swindle in history." Nettler (1978, p. 183) describes what happened:

> The motive for this series of official deceits was not the ordinary one of getting something for nothing. It is not alleged that the officials responsible for New York's financial disaster stole money. The major motive was political—to get into office and to stay there. A minor motive may have been "to do good." The impulse toward bankruptcy was well expressed by one of New York's mayors, Robert Wagner, who declared in his budget speech of 1965 that "I do not propose to permit our fiscal problems to set the limits of our commitments to meet the essential needs of the people of this city" (Auletta 1975b, p. 29).
>
> Ten years later New York City owed investors in its bonds $54 *billion*. Some 160,000 people who had bought city securities stood to lose their money, and the interest costs on the city's debt alone were running at almost one-fourth of its expense budget (Auletta 1975a, p. 38).
>
> This financial fiasco was lubricated with fraud. In simplest terms, urban officials misrepresented the financial status of their city when they went to borrow money. They claimed collateral they did not have. In July and August of 1975, State Comptroller Arthur Levitt noted that city officers listed as collateral "$324 *million* in fictitious state and federal aid [and] overstated by a staggering $408.3 *million* the real-estate taxes it could expect to collect" (Auletta 1975a, p. 38, emphasis added).

"Creative accounting" produces wealth out of nothing and it is endlessly manipulable. For example, in 1972 a director of the city's off-track betting listed its earnings at $25 million. Other officials arbitrarily raised the number to $50 million. Real earnings were $14 million. In February, 1975, a young lawyer working for one of New York City's creditors, Bankers' Trust, discovered that the city did not have tax receipts legally required to underwrite its sale of $260 million in bonds. And the chronicle of deceit goes on.

Auletta (1979) compares the city's practice of forecasting its revenues on nothing tangible with the classic swindle of selling interests in what one does not have. There is another parallel with theft in business. Governments commit fraud for the same reason some embezzlers steal: They live in higher style than they can afford. Uluschak's cartoon makes the point.

"Just as I suspected — the government's living beyond our means!"

Reproduced by permission of artist Uluschak and *The Edmonton Journal.* © 1980 (February 27).

Another Road

Promising to make things better by having others pay for what one decrees paves another road to urban bankruptcy and political fraud. The mayor of New York City, Edward Koch (1980), describes the financial difficulties imposed on a city when it accepts federal aid to augment "social service" programs.

"Those who pay the piper call the tune" and cities find themselves subject to commandments from distant legislators and bureaucrats who are *not responsible for the costs of their orders. Koch writes:*

> By the close of the 1970's, the cities found themselves under the guns of dozens of federal laws imposing increasingly draconian mandates. From the perspective of local government the mandate mandarins who write these laws appear to be guided by certain disturbing maxims, such as:
>
> **1.** *Mandates solve problems, particularly those in which you are not involved.* The federal government, for example, has shown no reluctance in ordering sweeping changes, the impact of which it will never have to face since it does not hold the final service-delivery responsibilities in such areas as education, transportation, and sewage disposal.
>
> **2.** *Mandates need not be tempered by the lessons of local experience.* Frequently, a statutory directive will impose a single nationwide solution to a perceived problem. . . .
>
> **3.** *Mandates will spontaneously generate the technology required to achieve them.*
>
> **4.** *The price tag of the lofty aspiration to be served by a mandate should never deter its imposition upon others* (pp. 43–44, emphasis his).

Koch's essay documents the irrationality of federal commandments to cities concerning transportation and education of the handicapped, ocean pollution, housing, public assistance, civil service appointments, and civil service pensions. It is easy to *order* the world to be better than it is if one does not have to pay the costs of implementation. But, decrees are not the performances they dictate, and corruption is built into extravagant ends sought without heed to available means.

Implications

New York City is not the only government to have been committed to deceitful financing by the demands of democratic politics. Other cities are in similar predicaments and so are federal governments. Atrill (1979) provides examples of ways in which Canadian economic entities—corporations and governments—can misrepresent their financial conditions by changing definitions of "payables" and "receivables." A former Secretary of the United States Treasury, William Simon (1978) confirms Atrill's examples. Simon writes:

> The governmental statement of the federal debt was grossly deceptive. Enormous liabilities were not listed on the budget at all but were described as off budget items. Consequently, the citizens rarely realized the magnitude of the government debt.
>
> The missing off budget items themselves were staggering. By 1975 $11 billion was owed by "independent" agencies like the TVA and the Export-Import Bank. Government-sponsored enterprises, such as the Farm Credit Administration and the Federal Home Loan Board, owed $88 billion. . . . But the biggest and still growing obligation was Social Security, estimated at more than $4 trillion—a figure which did not include Civil Service and other pensions (p. 91)
>
> Deficit spending . . . generated its own pathological form of "bookkeeping." Politicians discovered that they could launch federal programs and win the enthusiastic support of grateful voters without taking a penny out of the Treasury. As every obligation fell due, all the government had to do was to sell new bonds to replace the old ones. As government borrowing became astronomical, a new "convention" in record keeping gradually emerged, and this also occurred on state and local levels of government; it consisted simply of hiding the true amount of the debt (p. 100).

Research by the accounting firm of W.M. O'Reilly and Company demonstrates how these "new conventions" in keeping the books conceal government debt. In January, 1980, President Carter estimated an American budget deficit of $16 billion and proposed a surplus by March of $16.5 billion. But, by summer, that estimate was revised again to a deficit of $30 billion and by October that had become $40 billion. However, the O'Reilly tally puts the federal deficit at more then ten times the official estimate—at $431 billion. Seligman (1980) explains:

> None of [the government's] numbers are realistic. If the federal government adopted accounting assumptions that are taken for granted in the real world, the deficits would always be much larger. [The O'Reilly study] makes one simple point about federal accounting practices: unlike the private sector, the Feds do not bring increases in accrued liabilities into the "expense" side of the income statement. [By contrast, the O'Reilly study] added in accrued pension costs and reserves for losses on federal loan guarantees. The O'Reilly accounting methods yield a cumulative four-year deficit of $1,024 trillion for 1977-1980.

The generality of findings such as those revealed by Atrill, Auletta, O'Reilly, Simon, and others indicates something generic to democratic politics.

Two implications can be drawn. The first is that good intentions do not in themselves produce benign results. As poets have long noted, the road to hell is paved with good intention. The conditions under which meaning to do good does social harm deserve description in another volume, but a general principle can be stated: Irresponsibility damages, and politics encourages irresponsibility.

To be responsible is to suffer (or enjoy) the consequences of one's acts. *To be irresponsible* is to transfer consequences to others. The transfer returns us to Hobbes's jungle in which each wars with all.

A second implication is that all forms of government carry seeds of their decay. Democracy has its own frailty. Its weakness lies in its tendency to convert statesmen into demagogues who promise great returns from small investments. Citizens are urged to vote themselves rewards from others' productivity. Democracy then becomes ochlocracy and it begins to fulfill the tyrant's prophecy, as when Fidel Castro (1971) calls "elections, parliaments, and freedom of the press . . . anachronisms . . . condemned by history."

Compared to the social harm wreaked by fraud in business and politics, robbery and sneak thievery are minor offenses. Varieties of theft by force and stealth are the topic of the next chapter.

4 THEFT BY FORCE AND STEALTH

Abstract • Robbery and sneak-thievery satisfy a complex of appetites, including desires for excitement, independence, property, and gratified hostility. • People are inhibited from adopting criminal means of satisfying these desires by training, talent, and cost. • A cost-benefit schedule for theft is suggested. • Some individual careers and some depictions of categories of robber, burglar, and sneak-thief illustrate rewards and costs of these larcenies. • Styles of talented thief and the peculiar hazards of their work are described. • Theft is shown to vary with opportunities to steal. ○ Increases in the quantity of portable wealth produce increases in theft. ○ This occurs more frequently as likely offenders meet suitable targets. Suitability of target includes vulnerability of property and vulnerability of victim.

ROBBERY AND SNEAK-THIEVERY ARE EXCITING. They are also rewarding, if "reward" includes the psychic satisfactions of adventure, independence, and gratified hostility as well as possible financial gain.

There is no reason, of course, why these pleasures cannot be mixed for any particular individual. No one acts from only one motive, as Dostoyevsky assured us. Furthermore, there is no reason why thieves should be all of one piece as regards their successes and failures. There are competent thieves and bunglers just as there are skillful architects and inept ones. However, to explain forceful and stealthy theft by their pleasures turns scholarly inquiry around. It changes the question from "Why do people steal?" to "Why don't more people steal more often?"

The answer to the second question has three crossed prongs. One part of the answer is that people are trained toward[1] a moral code that inhibits their taking others' property. A second facet of the answer is that people have different abilities, interests, and tastes. Strong-arm robbery requires a strong arm. Second-story burglary requires agility. Raffles-type thievery requires a social front. "Opportunity costs" intrude upon every vocation; doing this means that one

---

[1] Use of the preposition, "toward," indicates that we are trained in a direction, but that the training is a matter of degree. It is never complete.

cannot do that. Choice among opportunities reflects interests and preferences.

A third prong of the answer is that stealing, like any other pleasure, carries a cost, and that, for some people, given their training, their personalities, and their situations, the estimated cost exceeds the imagined gain.

Listing some of the costs and rewards of stealthy and forceful larcenies leads to descriptions of kinds of people engaged full- or part-time in such work. A cost-benefit schedule is outlined in Table 4.1.

EXCITEMENT, AUTONOMY, HOSTILITY

Most persons who work at robbery and burglary tell us that they enjoy the thrill of theft. Shoplifters differ in this regard in part because so many of them are impulsive, part-time thieves without a strong interest in the art of larceny. But those who mug people or burglarize private residences or business establishments regard their work as fun.

This is true of such unskillful, but successful, burglars as Charlie Manson's girls who enjoyed "creepy-crawly" forays into others' residences. It is also true of Mafiosi. One recently admitted, "I was born a thief. I enjoyed it. I went into the Mafia because I wanted to" (Teresa 1979).

This thief denied that he had ever been poor and that material deprivation had anything to do with his taste for theft and violence. A similar picture is provided by such skillful, yet frequently arrested, thieves as Willie "The Actor" Sutton.

Sutton

Willie Sutton committed his first burglary with his pal, Charlie McCarthy, when he was 10 just "to see if we could do it, that's all" (Sutton 1976, p. 23). He went on to other styles of theft before specializing in bank robbery, a crime he found gratifying. As Sutton tells it:

> I never had anything against stealing (p. 28). Why did I rob banks? Because I enjoyed it. I loved it. I was more alive when I was inside a bank, robbing it, than at any other time in my life. I enjoyed everything about it so much that one or two weeks later I'd be out looking for the next job. But to me the money was the chips, that's all. The winnings. I kept robbing banks when, by all logic, it was foolish. When it could cost me far more than I could possibly gain.
>
> Actually, I spent far more time planning how to break out of jails, if

Table 4.1 Cost-Benefit Schedule for Theft*

Costs	Benefits
Probability of being caught. This probability becomes a cost only when it is multiplied by individual weighing of the risk of being punished if caught and pricing of the "value" of that punishment. The value of punishment differs among individuals and differs in their assessment of the relative pains of such penalties as fine, time, shame, removal from familiar surroundings, and lost earnings if incarcerated.	Market value of stolen property when fenced plus money stolen.
	Use value of stolen property retained by thief.
	Tax freedom.
	Leisure: e.g., a burglar's work-week versus workweek of legal job available to thief.
Loss of legal income; time out from lawful occupation.	Job satisfaction: pleasure in one's work, self-employment satisfaction, excitement, pride in skills.
Loss of peripheral benefits of lawful work: paid vacation, medical insurance, pension contribution.	Security: freedom from risk of unemployment.
Job risks: accident, being wounded or killed.	Security: free room and board, free health care, aid to dependents, wages earned if imprisoned.
Job costs: learning skills and acquiring tools; payoffs to inside men and others; fencing.	Repute: as successful thief.
Work: casing and doing.	
Subjective costs: anxiety about getting caught and punished; fear of injury.	
Subjective costs of punishment: shame, guilt. How much does a specific fine hurt? How much does imprisonment hurt? How much are time and freedom worth?	
Damaged repute: as thief, or as unsuccessful thief if one is vocationally committed to stealing.	

*Costs and benefits are possible ones. They need not all pertain to a particular actor, and they may, of course, differ in actuality from an actor's judgment of them.

Reproduced, with modifications, from G. Nettler, *Explaining Crime*, Second edition, Table 10-1, with permission of the publisher. © 1978 by McGraw-Hill Book Company.

only because I spent so much more time inside, trying to get out, than outside, trying to get in. If any enterprising reporter had ever asked me why I broke out of jail, I suppose ... what I would have said [was] "Because I was in." But also, you know, because there's a thrill that comes from breaking out of jail, after years of the most meticulous planning, with everybody watching you, against all the odds, that is like nothing else in the world (pp. 120–121).

Sutton's description of the pleasures of his work parallels the excitement that lawful risk-takers describe—making a difficult rock-climb or hang-gliding. The excitement is sometimes sexual and, in the male in particular, we observe a varying association of risk with erotic stimulation.

Young men get erections from many presumably non-sexual stimuli, including driving at speed, hearing engines roar, climbing high in trees, setting fires, listening to martial music, and seeing flags fly (Barclay & Haber 1965, Hirschfeld 1956, Kinsey et al. 1948, 1953, Krafft-Ebing 1935, Sorensen 1973, Terman 1938). It is no surprise, then, that some burglars get erections while doing their sneak-thieving. But, with or without the sexual excitement, taking risks is fun. It is more fun for some individuals than for others, of course, and there are those who are shocked that people enjoy danger:

When two Englishmen named Frederick Slade and Yeats Brown announced in 1827 that they had just scaled the Jungfrau—and had done it simply for the fun of it—it was considered something of a scandal. Their honest lack of non-recreational justification for the expedition was seen as being somehow less than honorable, possibly even immoral in that it put human life in jeopardy without other rationalization (Johnson 1978, p. 102).

It is not just coincidence that the first men to climb the Bridalveil Ice Falls in Colorado compared their feeling with criminal success:

We howled and hollered. It was a little hokey, but we felt this incredible elation. Like we had just pulled off the crime of the century (Johnson 1978, p. 98).

Explaining how stealing came to be Willie Sutton's pleasure takes the same form as explanations people give for becoming mountain-climbers or accountants: Interests meet circumstances, where circumstances include particular people.

One of Sutton's wardens, Marvin Klein, visited him frequently in the Queen's County House of Detention and quizzed Willie about "how a man with my interests had become a thief ... [Klein] was such an unusually humane and intelligent man for his line of work that in short order I was asking how a man like him had become a warden" (p. 245).

Sutton calls the warden's story "interesting" and concludes that as many "accidents" determined the warden's career as the robber's.

Mesrine

None of the deprivations usually invoked to account for thievery explain many careers sincerely devoted to crime. Explanation reduces to description of personalities that enjoy the chase, the loot, the leisure, and the demands of their criminal work. This applies to Willie Sutton and also to that more dangerous French "supercrook," Jacques Mesrine.

Mesrine was born of rich parents. They may have been newly rich, as one prosecutor commented sneeringly, but young Jacques was reared in comfort. He grew up in a manor in the French countryside and attended expensive, private schools. He gave early indication of being a "bad boy," of resenting authority, and enjoying trickery and lying. He was expelled from a succession of good schools.

Mesrine was a charmer and smooth conversationalist in the style of successful psychopaths, and he was cruel. He boasted of his pleasure in torturing captured Algerian peasants when he was fighting with the O.A.S. (*Organisation Armée Secrète*). He had his picture taken, à la Bonnie and Clyde, staring from behind an automatic rifle (Schofield 1980). He discovered early on that he could kill without remorse and he bragged that he had murdered 39 people. One is not sure, of course, that he kept accurate score.

Mesrine was a master of disguise and a prankster in crime. While robbing the old millionaire, Michel Lelièvre, Mesrine took a picture of himself wearing a mask in the image of the French Communist leader, Georges Marchais. Mesrine was by then becoming a Leftist and his message was that his thefts were, like Communist expropriation of capitalists, justified.

Mesrine lived well and enjoyed the perennial pleasures of wine, women, and good food. He married and divorced twice, but "loved" many women all of whom seem to have been enchanted with his virility.

Mesrine kept in shape for his work and trained with the diligence of a professional athlete. He disciplined himself to overcome fear. He planned his crimes and took pride in being a master thief and escape artist. He often returned to the scene of a crime to make a second "score" on the assumption that no one would expect such boldness. He liked to rob establishments in his neighborhood on Friday afternoons because he thought that was his lucky day and because, as a fellow Parisian, he understood the urgency of police officials and other custodians to quit work early on the eve of a weekend.

He seduced a 19-year-old French-Canadian girl, fresh from her convent school near Montreal, and made her his mistress and partner in crime. His charm captivated her parents as well and they seem not to have objected to their daughter's life with so attractive and successful a man.

As so often happens with smart thieves, Mesrine was undone by an accomplice. One of his associates in robbery, Charly Bauer, was living with a female schoolteacher who served Charly as mistress, political indoctrinator, and driver. Police had traced the registration of the teacher's automobile, found it parked on a street in Mesrine's neighborhood, and, from that clue, cornered Mesrine as he was driving off on a Friday afternoon for his weekend in the country. Some 21 bullets ended Mesrine's career at age 42.

The romance of Big Crime is again illustrated by the fact that Mesrine has been adopted as a hero by some punk-rockers and defended as a revolutionary by some Leftist intellectuals (Cobb 1980).

Lessons

We cannot explain Mesrine and Sutton in any scientific sense of "explanation." We can only describe them and comprehend their motives.

Their careers illustrate our themes. The constancy of appetites and interests is striking—from childhood to manhood. None of the causes usually invoked to explain devotion to crime apply. Neither man suffered poverty or lack of opportunity for legitimate work. Neither suffered from a discordant family, parental rejection, or inadequate schooling. In Mesrine's case, in particular, his father remained devoted to him even after he became a notorious thief and killer. These Big Thieves suffered—if that is the word—only from personalities that detested routine work and loved excitement, easy money, good food, drink, and sexy women.

We learn from the lives of Mesrine and Sutton the repetitive lesson that careers are made by more than environments. We also learn that personalities guide lives, but in ways that elude the psychologist's coarse net of regularities.

We learn, too, that ideas are justifications or epiphenomena[2] as

---

[2] "*Epiphenomenalism:* The doctrine that consciousness is merely an epiphenomenon of physiological processes, and that it has no power to affect these processes" (*Random House Dictionary of the English Language,* © 1966 by Random House, Inc., publishers, and reproduced by permission).

well as motives. We become skeptical, then, of the adequacy of verbalization as representation of thought and we are skeptical of the *independent* power of ideas as causes of acts. Mesrine, like Giangi Feltrinelli (Chapter 11, Volume Two), covered his actions with ideologies—Fascist first, Communist later. These ideas were in the air; they were congenial. They accompanied the personalities that generated their crimes.

Belson's Boys

Vignettes such as these from robber's lives match the characterization of more persistent young thieves revealed by extensive interviews with English boys. Belson and his associates (1975) talked with 1,425 youths, 13 to 16 years of age, in London. Their inquiry was conducted in a way that protected the anonymity of the boys and varied the interview so as to increase the validity of respondents' confessions of theft.

A significant difference between more and less larcenous boys is the greater desire for "fun and excitement" expressed by the more delinquent youths. Moreover, the boys who said they did not have enough fun and excitement were also the ones who wanted more of these pleasures and who found that stealing provided them.

The pleasures of thieving are more than the joys of taking risks and gaining loot. They also include the satisfaction of venting hostility.

Hostility

The joy of expressed hatred runs with the other pleasures of sneak-thievery and robbery. Sources of hatred vary, of course, and they do not always lie in having been hated, although that is a common origin.

Hatred of self and hatred of others frequently go hand-in-hand and their roots are often well-concealed. For example, Willie Sutton can find no causes of his being "set against society" (p. 28), but he has no doubt that he was—early on. Envy was also there, but that is a common emotion. Willie's first job, at age 15, was in a bank and he hated the looks of its president:

> The bank president would be driven up in his limousine, his chauffeur would open the door for him, and in he would come—morning clothes, derby hat, cane hooked over his arm—nodding at everybody without looking at anybody—and it infuriated me (p. 18).

Theft is one technique for satisfying hatred. It satisfies hostility in children who steal from their parents and teachers. It satisfies it in lonely, older women—like the faded movie star—who steal junk from cosmetic counters. It satisfies it in robbers who like to see fear in their victims. Thus a well-spoken bank robber tells us:

> My mania for power, socially, sexually, and otherwise can feel no degree of satisfaction until I feel sure I have struck the ultimate of submission and terror in the minds and bodies of my victims. . . . It's very difficult to explain all the queer, fascinating sensations pounding and surging through me while I'm holding a gun on a victim, watching his body tremble and sweat . . . . This is the moment when all the rationalized hypocrisies of civilization are suddenly swept away and two men stand there facing each other morally and ethically naked, and right and wrong are the absolute commands of the man behind the gun (cited by Barzun 1962, p. 186).

Robbery, more than burglary, gratifies the lust for power that appeases hatred. When Saul Bellow's ancient *Mr. Sammler* (1970) observes a big, black dude mugging people on New York buses, the thief follows Sammler, catches him in the vacant lobby of his apartment building, and pins the old man against the wall with one arm. With the other, he takes out his penis and makes Sammler look at it. The organ is a weapon, a symbol of power. Nothing is said. Sammler understands the gesture.

Bellow's story is fiction, but it is true.

GAIN

It is obvious that people steal to get wealth, but gain is relative. It is relative to the actual costs of an enterprise and to the psychic importance of those costs. It is relative to a person's expectations and opportunities, where opportunities again are both objectively identifiable and subjectively appreciated.

Gain from theft, like gain from lawful work, depends on job skills. Just as few tennis pros or opera singers make "the big time," so few thieves make "big scores." Most thieves, and particularly young ones, have little talent for any vocation, including that of theft. They earn little whether they work legally or illegally.

Forty-Nine Armed Robbers

The vocational talent of run-of-the-street robbers is illustrated in research by Petersilia, Greenwood, and Lavin (1978). These investigators interviewed 49 men serving prison terms in California for armed robbery. These offenders averaged 39 years of age, had completed an average of eight years schooling, and were, for the most part (80%), of "normal or bright-normal" intelligence. On the average, they committed their first serious crime when they were 14 years old and were first arrested one year later. Most of these robbers were incarcerated at least once before they were 18 years old. The majority had experienced broken homes, low socioeconomic status, and criminal siblings and associates.

As workers in crime and in legitimate jobs, these men were incompetent. About half depended on lawful work for their usual source of income, but their pay was low. Another 10 percent showed no interest at any time in regular work. When these men turned to crime, they rarely specialized or developed skill. Their usual careers started with juvenile auto theft and burglary and graduated to adult robbery and forgery. The researchers write:

> The majority said they had switched to robbery because it required little preparation and few tools, was easy to do, seldom required hurting anyone, and offered unlimited potential targets. Also, robbery could be committed alone, eliminating the risk of being implicated by a partner. The offenders saw "take" as the primary influencing factor in deciding whether or not to commit a certain crime, the risks involved being secondary (Petersilia et al. 1978, p. vii).

Most of these robbers worked at crime without plan. What little planning they did involved visiting the crime site and, sometimes, staking out the target. Sixty percent said they were under the influence of drugs or alcohol while doing their criminal work and that desire for money for these comforting chemicals was the principal motive for theft.

These men returned to crime soon after their release from jails or prisons and were arrested again within three to five months after resuming criminal activity.

Given the low risk overall of thefts resulting in arrests, and arrests resulting in imprisonment, these career thieves are failures. At the peak of their criminal work, they were averaging only a few thousand dollars a year from their thefts.

Shoplifters

A similar pattern of low material gain characterizes the more sporadic work of shoplifters. Those who are apprehended usually have taken items of low value and, as far as we can tell, have not been well rewarded during the span of their careers in crime. Kirkwood (1977) reports that Canadian shoplifters on the average have $28. worth of stolen property on them when apprehended. Warner's (1979) analysis of theft in a large Edmonton department store shows that 85 percent of arrested thieves had stolen things totaling less than $50.

The fact that individuals gain little from shoplifting should not be interpreted to mean that the loss to stores is small. Given the numbers of thieves and repetition of their crimes, losses to stores may be considerable. For example, it is estimated that "unexplained inventory shrinkage" or "the five-finger discount" accounts for four to five percent of the value of sporting goods sales (Harbin 1979).

The kind of person who sneak-thieves from retail shops varies with location and the the kind of store studied. People steal the kinds of things they tend to buy (Warner 1979). Thus thieves in drug stores, pinching candy and cigarettes, tend to be younger than thieves in grocery and department stores. Thieves in sports shops tend to be young men, taking the kind of equipment they use. In supermarkets, apprehended shoplifters are disproportionately women (Won & Yamamoto 1968).

However, all characterizations of shoplifters need to be qualified by the fact that investigators do not ordinarily compare attributes of apprehended thieves with attributes of populations *at risk*. Comparisons are usually made with representation in the population at large. Such comparisons may be inappropriate since the general population does not shop in different kinds of stores in numbers equal to their proportions. For example, women disproportionately frequent grocery and department stores; young men disproportionately frequent sporting goods stores. A fair comparison of the probability of theft by "kind of person" would relate numbers of those apprehended to a population base of numbers at risk.

Warner (1979) attempted to control for "population at risk" by making periodic door-tallies of the characteristics of entrants. In making this check, Warner corrects the common idea that shoplifters in department stores are disproportionately female. His door count found only one-third of shoppers in Bigstore to be men, but men accounted for 60 percent of those arrested. This disproportion is produced principally by young men, particularly those in the 15- to 19-year age group.

Boosters and Snitches

In her early study of apprehended shoplifters in one Chicago department store, Cameron (1964) suggested that most such thieves were "snitches," impulsive and unskilled pilferers with no stigmata differentiating them from the run-of-the-store shopper. However, some small minority of shoplifters may be "boosters," people with a vocational interest in stealing who develop particular skills in thievery and who may work in small groups.

Warner (1979) encountered no such "professional thieves" during his surveillance of Bigstore in Canada. What little we know of such thieves comes from detectives' reports and confidential interviews with admitted boosters. No tallies of their financial gain are available and we do not know how much boosting is vocational or only avocational.

Summary

International research on shoplifting tells us a few things about this common larceny:

1. Most shoplifting goes undetected and unreported when detected. Blankenburg (1976) had his aides steal things in a department store and a chain of supermarkets in West Germany. He finds that less than 10 percent of their thefts were noticed and that, when noticed, both sales personnel and other customers were reluctant to do anything. The proportion of shoppers who steal is small, however. Hughes (1974) reports a study in which four American stores were saturated with detectives for one day. These guards attempted to follow all customers while they were in stores. Of 1,647 shoppers under surveillance, 109 were observed to have stolen at least once.

2. Thieves, particularly young ones, continue to steal after they are apprehended if they are not otherwise punished.

Wisher (1974) was able to interview apprehended juvenile shoplifters. He reports that 85 percent of these young men and 62 percent of young women stole again after their first discovery. Kraut (1976) seconds Wisher's findings and holds that "the average apprehended shoplifter stole over five times after apprehension."

These results run counter to an established doctrine in criminology that says that snitches desist after arrest. Cameron so argues, but her data do not allow her conclusion.

3. Common stories of kleptomania and of compulsive theft in menopausal women have little substance. Most shoplifting cannot be explained by Freudian ideas of the sexual significance of the objects stolen or by neurotic needs.

Kleptomania is defined as "a morbid impulse to steal" or as "pathological stealing" (Hinsie & Campbell 1960), and the term is usually applied to theft of trivial or useless things. Theft of worthless objects in itself makes the stealing less rational and more neurotic.

Among psychoanalysts kleptomania derives from "emotional starvation" during infancy and represents a repressed wish. What that

wish is depends on the psychoanalyst. Staub (1962), for example, regards such theft as expressing penis envy; Stekel (1943) thinks such
theft is a substitute for deprived sexual gratification; and Adler (1917)
sees such theft as an attempt to gain power, where the compulsion to
be powerful is stimulated by infantile rejection.

Criminologists are forever hearing tales of rich little-old-ladies
known to be kleptomaniacs and whose thefts are permitted by sympathetic shopkeepers and paid for by understanding husbands or
sons. There may be such cases, but none have been verified. As far as
we know, the overwhelming bulk of shoplifting is done by "normal"
people who steal what they would ordinarily buy and use.

4. Stores in university areas in the United States are particularly
vulnerable to shoplifting. Kirkwood (1977) estimates that retail stores
in such districts suffer about three times the amount of theft as similar
stores in other neighborhoods. This fact, if replicated, cautions
against inferring a necessary association of theft with poverty and low
levels of schooling.

5. As with other unskillful thefts, there is a tendency for apprehended shoplifters to be disproportionately represented by ethnic
"minorities."[3]

In West Germany, Blankenburg (1976) reports that "foreigners"
are overrepresented among apprehended thieves. In Hawaii, Won
and Yamamoto (1968) find Hawaiians to be apprehended far in ex-
cess of their numbers in the population while Japanese, the largest
ethnic group in the islands, are greatly underrepresented among
shoplifters. Caucasians appear as thieves in proportion to their numbers in Hawaii.

In eastern Canada, Normandeau (1971) finds French-Canadians significantly overrepresented among apprehended shoplifters in six
Montreal department stores. In western Canada, Warner (1979) observes that Indian, Inuit, and Metis shoppers are disproportionately
arrested for shoplifting.

6. All generalizations about the nature of shoplifters should be interpreted with caution because of the variability in law enforcement
among stores, within cities, and among countries (Blankenburg 1976,
Rojek 1979).

---

[3] "Minorities" is placed in quotation marks because the term in its sociological sense no longer refers to proportions, but rather to some conception
of deprivation or subordination. Thus women are sometimes considered to
be a "minority" although they constitute a numerical majority. Similarly,
French-Canadians in Quebec are sometimes accorded "minority" status despite their overwhelming majority in that province.

Inside Thieves

One of the easiest ways to steal, and most profitable, is to take property where one works. This need not be embezzlement, a violation of financial trust. It is most frequently sneak-thievery, and it may be theft from employers or from customers.

It is estimated that "internal thieves" steal more per thief than do robbers and burglars (Kirkwood 1977) and that the ratio of internal to external theft in the United States and Canada runs about five to one (Parker 1977).

If inventory losses are correctly calculated, it is probable that the amounts stolen by American employees doubled every two years during the 1970s (Parker 1977). The value of such theft is placed at about $10 *billion* a year (Deloatch & Roach 1977), but this is only an informed guess.

Norman Jaspan (1960), the head of an engineering consulting firm, reports that "in more than 50 percent of assignments involving engineering projects with no hint of dishonesty, white collar crime was uncovered. In addition [in 1959 alone] our staff has unearthed more than $60 million worth of dishonesty with more than 60 percent attributable to supervisory and executive personnel" (p. 10). More recently, Jaspan (1970) said he believed that companies in Canada and the United States suffer a "better than 50 percent chance" of being victims of "sizable dishonesty."

The North American construction industry estimates that between one and two percent of the value of its equipment is stolen each year. These thefts range from hand tools and building materials to diesel tractors. One electrician explained his thievery by the necessities of inflation that make it profitable for him to "moonlight" on weekend jobs. He installs wiring for referred customers at less than the going rate because he steals the equipment from the construction sites where he works during the week.

People who handle money and other property are in prime position to steal. Canadian and American banks estimate that about 80 percent of the amounts stolen from them are taken by their employees. Bank robbery is a relatively minor source of loss.

Similarly, baggage handlers in airports have an easy time stealing from luggage or taking likely looking bags. The crime is so common in some areas that London's Heathrow Airport has come to be known as "Thiefrow" by insiders who steal about $15 million a year (Moynahan 1978). Successful rifling of luggage is called "the lucky dip" and, with the ingenuity that characterizes bright thieves, new modes of effecting the lucky dip are invented. Thus Fernand Romain, an employee in Paris's Orly Airport, developed the technique of having himself loaded onto Air France flights in a packing case. This gave him unlimited time to "faire le lucky dip" before climbing back into his case before landing. On a recent flight Romain stole about $44,000 worth of gems. All this we now know because an envious co-worker turned him in (Moynahan 1980).

Burglary

Burglary differs from "inside theft" by requiring trespass onto another's property in order to steal. In common law, burglary was defined as breaking into and entering another's dwelling at night with the intention of committing a felony. Today, however, burglary in most jurisdictions refers to theft from another person's territory, day or night, with or without forcible entry, and from any part of another's property, be it dwelling, factory, office, or garage. One can even burglarize gardens, as Herb Caen (1978) notes:

> SANFRANCISCAENA: ... What's going on in Presidio Heights, that toney arrondissement between Presidio and Arguello? Plantnaping! And in the dead of night. The rascal is a divorcee with a famous triple-gaited name who, wielding a vicious trowel, has been hitting the mansions of the mighty (Getty, Davies, Lewis, Hills, Hellman, the old Alice Griffith property) and carting off plants in a wheelbarrow. Thousands of bucks worth ... Everybody's being nice, since her mother is the grandest of dames, but the Haul of Justice can't be stalled forever (© 1978 by the *San Francisco Chronicle*. Reproduced by permission).

In American cities, Reppetto (1974) finds that about half of the burglaries are from residences and that the overwhelming majority of residential burglaries are committed while their occupants are away.

The typical burglar is a sneak thief who wishes to avoid confrontation with his or her victim. However, an occasional burglary—about one in 100 in American cities—turns into robbery when thief unexpectedly meets victim (Reppetto 1974, p. 5).

The average "take" per offense is greater for burglars than for street robbers, in a ratio of about three to two, and the value of property taken in each incident is relatively little. In recent years, the average residential burglary produces a loss to the victim of about $400., not all of which is net to the thief since some property is fenced. Of course, the total amount stolen by burglars is large because of the number of thieves and the low ratio of arrests to crimes. In Toronto, one-third of burglaries are not reported to the police (Waller & Okihiro 1978). Reppetto (1974, p. 4) believes that "if the number of unreported residential burglaries were taken into account, the total annual loss could be estimated in the vicinity of one billion dollars."

The majority of burglars in Western countries, like the majority of robbers, are young, unskillful men. In the United States, urban burglars are disproportionately nonwhite, and the nonwhites, when compared with other burglars, have a higher rate of previous offenses as indicated by both official records and self-reports (Pope 1977, Reppetto 1974, pp. 13–14).

With exceptions to be noted below, burglars have neither criminal nor lawful job skills. Of 97 convicted burglars whom Reppetto interviewed, 80 percent had never earned more than $200. a week in a legitimate job. Nearly 70 percent of these Boston burglars were drug-users and Reppetto concludes that burglary rates would be reduced if addiction could be cured or legally gratified.

Young burglars and female burglars tend to steal in groups; solo thievery is more characteristic of older and more talented burglars. The typical unskillful burglar does not travel far to commit his or her crime. White thieves avoid black neighborhoods and blacks are wary of police patrols in white neighborhoods. Most burglars choose victims by their accessibility. Thus well-guarded, expensive apartments are relatively secure from young thieves and are chosen only by older, more professional burglars who are tempted by the greater value of property in such locations. In Boston, Reppetto found "luxury high rise apartment areas [characterized by] elaborate security precautions" to have low burglary rates and no robberies (p. 46).

Accessibility also determines theft in rural areas. In remote districts, burglars have an easy job because property is unguarded and proprietors trusting. Barber's (1976) study of specialists in rural theft found these thieves to be cautious and ingenious. They choose victims carefully, "case" locations, and move property—cattle, for example—some distance before fencing it. Many of Barber's burglars regarded themselves as kinds of businessmen who denied that their crimes hurt anyone since insurance presumably compensated their victims.

Talented Thieves

The difference between a talented thief and the mediocre majority of robbers and burglars is like the difference between Bjorn Borg and a Sunday tennis hacker. The difference is a matter of "natural talent," but it is also a matter of practice and discipline.

John Mack (1972, Mack & Kerner 1975) reports on what he calls "able criminals" whom he got to know in Scotland through years of developed contacts. Mack is interested principally in men who make crime their only work and who develop specialized skills. He finds such talented thieves to have come from the same socioeconomic environment as less competent thieves, but to differ psychologically from these "textbook crooks" in their greater intelligence, emotional stability, planfulness, and financial gain. Successful thieves differ from inept ones in many of the same psychological attributes that mark differences between successful and failed businessmen, lawyers, or professors.

Mack's skillful criminals also differ from ordinary thieves in their greater ability to stay out of jail. Mack estimates that his talented Scots spend about one-eighth of their adult lives incarcerated compared with common robber-burglars who may spend as much as 60 percent of their prime years in prison. Given this freedom and their rationality in crime, Mack indicates that talented criminals generally make much more money than they would in those lawful occupations that are open to them. They make more money and they spend it. They live "high on the hog."

Example: MacLean

Talent, to be fulfilled, specializes. Specialization characterizes Mack's able criminals and others who engage in successful larcenous careers.

John Arthur MacLean's thieving illustrates the advantages of intelligence, planning, and a practiced mode of working at crime. MacLean is alleged to have committed 2,000 expensive burglaries on the American East Coast before he was caught at 33 years of age. "Super-thief," as he has been called, does not know when he began stealing, but he estimates that he was taking about $50,000. a week during his prime. Police think he may have grossed $133 million. Detective Arthur McLellan of the Fort Lauderdale Police Department believes MacLean may have been "the most successful burglar in history."

MacLean acquired many of the symbols of success. At the height of his career, he owned a Hughes 300C helicopter, a Lake seaplane, a Cessna 172 modified to carry a trail bike, a high speed motorboat, and several fast cars and motorcycles.

MacLean's specialty was electronics. He was a master of burglar alarms and a student of police behavior. He tuned in on police radios to get information on reports of stolen goods before fencing his own loot. Like many able thieves, MacLean enjoyed playing the game of cops and robbers. Like Sutton and Mesrine, he was a skillful actor. Tom Zito (1980) describes MacLean's pleasure in his work:

> After he once penetrated a home with an open-line telephone alarm (which requires the user to call in after returning home), the alarm company routinely called the house, thinking that the subscribers themselves had forgotten to report in.

Superthief knew he would have to produce a code number, so he says he instead answered the phone in a baby's voice: "Hello, is this Daddy? Do you want Mummy? Mummy's on the potty." He set the phone down, continued burglarizing the house, and finally came back to say, "Mummy still can't come to the phone but she says to tell you this house has just been burglarized."

Such was his sense of humor. He would glue old sets of dentures to doorknobs, short sheet beds, empty bullets from self-defense weapons found in drawers and leave them—chambers open—arranged in symmetrical rows in conspicuous places. If he considered the amount of jewelry he found too insignificant ... to take, he would set the gems on the kitchen table and steal the control panel of the victim's burglar alarm instead. He says he often left telephone books open to the appropriate page, the police department listing circled with the notation, "Call this number" (© 1980 by the *Washington Post.* Reproduced by permission).

MacLean was caught because he changed his mode of operation. Faced with a safe he could not open, and challenged by this vocational problem, MacLean consulted his fence. The fence suggested three thieving associates with the requisite skills and MacLean, against his better judgment, accepted the cooperative assignment. Despite rehearsal, one of the gang left a walkie-talkie radio at the crime scene and diligent detective work traced the instrument to MacLean.

Police found about one million dollars in cash and jewelry in MacLean's house. With immunity from prosecution granted them, MacLean's partners and his girlfriend testified against him and MacLean was sentenced to 15 years in prison.

Example: Raffles

A rare, but successful, style of burglar has been fictionalized in the character, "Raffles" (Hornung 1969). A Raffles-type burglar specializes in looting rich victims with whom he becomes acquainted in resorts. In the days of the great ocean liners, he also worked those floating hotels.

"Raffles's" talent lies in knowing languages, in being charming, and in playing the games of the resorts he frequents—riding, skiing, golf, tennis, bridge. He has "front"—appropriate costume and a presumed source of income "back home." He travels alone, usually, and is thus eligible to complete a hostess's table or make a party interesting. His welcome in affluent social circles allows him to size up victims and plan large thefts. His net gain is considerably reduced by his need for a fence and by the expenses of his front. However, since he enjoys the front, he does not regard it as a professional expense but rather as one of the benefits of his vocation.

No one knows how many thieves follow this larcenous road, but they must be few. The one I have known had a criminal career that lasted about 10 years. He felt he could have gone on forever, but he made the mistake of confiding in a girlfriend after long discipline in keeping himself private. When he tried to break off the affair, she blew the whistle.

Vocational Hazards

Partnerships are the most difficult business arrangement—more so than single ownership or corporate management. This pertains to criminal work as well as lawful work.

Working partners and loved ones constitute a hazard for able criminals. The most successful thieves are probably the solo, silent ones who develop a particular mode of operation and keep at it quietly. But most of us do not live alone and a weakness of even skillful criminals is the company they keep. Characteristically they become involved with a succession of unreliable women and shaky colleagues. Someone "flashes" his new wealth, or gets drunk and brags, or fights with his love, and such events repeatedly bring the thief to justice.

The trouble with thieves is that they lead disorderly lives. If they lived as soberly as, say, accountants, they might make a decent living out of stealing. But, whether crime "pays" for them depends, again, on the rate at which these actors individually discount the pains of their work from their pleasures.

CRIME AND OPPORTUNITY

People move in and out of careers as their peculiar personalities meet opportunities. Opportunity, we have said, is both objectively observable and subjectively appreciated. If we count objective opportunities for theft, and exclude for the moment individual differences in appreciation of those chances, we come to a commonsensical generalization: *More people steal as more things are available for theft at low cost.*

Cost is, again, a composite of conceived and actual risk of apprehension, risk of punishment if apprehended, quality and severity of punishment, and subjective judgment of the pain of that penalty.

Economists who explain crime usually count the objective costs and benefits of such work and pay little attention to the psychic satisfactions. They recognize that there are such, but they find subjective factors difficult to measure. With this qualification, economists agree with our generalization.

Economists assume that individuals supply a "product"—crime, in the present case—if there is demand for it. Demand may flow from other persons than suppliers, or from the same person who does the supplying (Vandaele 1978, p. 309).

Supply varies with opportunity costs (what it pays to do other things), with skills, and with costs imposed by the "crime prevention sector." This "model" of crime production has been tested in a variety of ways and a summary of this research can be read in Heineke (1978a) and Nettler (1978). The bulk of econometric assessment of crime confirms such popular assumptions as these:

1. The *probability* of punishment reduces the supply of crime.

2. *Severity* of punishment also reduces the supply of crime, but not so dramatically as does the probability of apprehension and penalty.

One should assume a threshold effect here. There may be some level of punishment, for some actors, below which punishment is ineffective. Similarly, there may be some level of pain that will deter people who are tempted to steal. However, such a level may be beyond that which a people's morality will tolerate.

3. The more things available for theft, and the greater the value of those objects relative to wealth that may otherwise be gained, the greater the supply of crime.

Heineke (1978b, p. 198) concludes from his survey of research that "lowering 'the take' . . . will have larger deterrent effects than the corresponding increases in probabilities of apprehension and conviction or increases in sentence lengths." However, McPheters (1976) shows that there is an interaction between size of "the take" and probability of punishment. As the probability of arrest and conviction declined for armed robbers in the United States, 1959 through 1971, more "marginal robbers" were drawn into this work so that their per caput gain decreased. In short, the "wage rate" of robbery declined, but it was still sufficiently high, given the low probability of penalty, to attract what might be called "moonlighters" in theft.

4. Theft increases as "likely offenders" (young men, for example) meet "suitable targets." Suitable targets include unguarded property and vulnerable individuals.

Cohen and Felson (1979) and Cohen, Felson, and Land (1980) relate American rates of theft to changes in styles of life that move activities away from households and hence make domiciles more vulnerable to thieves. Reduction in the density of population on sites where primary groups normally reside increases opportunity for theft, as does an increase in the proportion of adults living alone. Furthermore, an increase in the quantity and value of portable wealth produces increases in theft. Cohen and his colleagues interpret their findings in the context of changes in "routine activities" that open opportunities for theft.

A parallel conclusion is reached by Camp (1967) in his study of changes in bank robberies in the United States. Camp finds that, as banks became more open and unguarded, their robbers changed from professionals to part-time and unskillful thieves. Bringing tellers out from behind cages and eliminating armed guards made the new style of bank more inviting to untrained robbers.

Studies of victims add support to the assumption that crimes increase as likely offenders meet suitable targets. Hindelang and his associates (1978) analyze extensive American data from reports of victimization and find that crime clusters:

(a) Both *individuals* and *households* that have once been victimized are vulnerable to further depredation.

(b) Persons who live in households in which another member has been personally victimized are themselves at risk.

(c) Individuals who live in *households* that have been victimized are themselves vulnerable to crime.

In sum, people who live among criminals and share their demographic characteristics are likely to be prey to the crimes of their associates. Where one lives and how one lives affect the kind and amount of crime she or he suffers. Not surprisingly, the more time one spends in public places and among strangers, the greater the likelihood of being a victim of crime. Conversely, and unsurprisingly, the Hindelang group tell us (p. 262) that "individuals who have the ability to isolate themselves from those with offender characteristics" are relatively immune to criminal predation.

Our excursion through some criminal careers has been long and yet incomplete. It ends with comments on ways of responding to crime, the subject of Volume Four.

REFERENCES

ABC-TV. 1980. "Report on the Moscow Olympics." (July 30).

Abramson, L.Y. & H.A. Sackeim. 1977. "A paradox in depression: Uncontrollability and self-blame." *Psych.Bull.,* 84:838–851.

Adams, J.R. 1979. "Drawing the line in Cleveland." *Wall St.Jour.* 101:10 (Aug. 17).

———. 1980. "Chicago hangs on by its nails." *Wall St. Jour.,* 102:24 (Feb. 21).

Adler, A. 1917. *The Neurotic Constitution.* Trans. by B. Blueck and J.E. Lind. New York: Moffat, Yard.

Andenaes, J. 1952. "General prevention: Illusion or reality?" *Jour.Crim.Law, Criminol., & Police Sci.,* 43:176–198.

———. 1966. "The general preventive effects of punishment." *Univ.Penn.Law Rev.,* 114:949–983.

———. 1974. *Punishment and Deterrence.* Ann Arbor: Univ.Mich.Press.

Aronson, E. & D.R. Mettee. 1968. "Dishonest behavior as a function of differential levels of induced self-esteem." *Jour.Person.Soc. Psych.,* 9:121–127.

Arrow, K.J. 1974. *The Limits of Organization.* New York: Norton.

———. 1978. *Social Choice and Individual Values.* 2nd ed., New Haven: Yale U.P.

Associated Press. 1979. "Vexed him with lawsuits, she's guilty of barratry." (June 19).

Atrill, V. 1979. *How All Economies Work: Principles and Applications of Objective Economics.* Toronto: Dimensionless Science Publications.

Auletta, K. 1975a. "Who's to blame for the fix we're in?" *New York,* 8:29–41 (Oct. 27).

———. 1975b. "Should these men go to jail?" *New York,* 8:36–41 (Dec. 1).

———. 1979. *The Streets Were Paved With Gold.* New York: Random House.

Austin, R.L. 1978. "Intelligence and adolescent theft: A multiple indicator solution." *Crim.Justice & Beh.,* 5:211–226.

Ausubel, D.P. 1958. *Drug Addiction: Physiological, Psychological, and Sociological Aspects.* New York: Random House.

Bacon, D.C. 1976. "Ripoffs: New American way of life." *U.S. News & World Report,* 80:29–32 (May 31).

Baden, J. 1977. "A primer for the management of common pool resources." In G. Hardin & J. Baden (eds.), *Managing the Commons.* San Francisco: Freeman.

Baden, J. & R. Stroup. 1977. "Property rights, environmental quality, and the management of national forests." In G. Hardin & J. Baden (eds.), *Managing the Commons.* San Francisco: Freeman.

Bailey, W.C. 1980. "Deterrence and the celerity of the death penalty: A neglected question in deterrence research." *Soc.Forces,* 58:1308–1333.

Bailey, W.C. and R.P. Lott. 1976. "Crime, punishment, and personality: An examination of the deterrence question." *Jour.Crim.Law & Crim.,* 67:49–109.

Banfield, E.C. 1958. *The Moral Basis of a Backward Society.* New York: Free Press.

Barber, R.M. 1976. *The Professional Style of Rural Thieves and their Vocabularies of Motive.* Ph.D. dissertation. Columbus: Ohio State University.

Barbu, Z. 1951. "Studies in children's honesty." *Quart.Bull.Br. Psych.Soc.,* 2:53–57.

Barclay, A.M. & R.N. Haber. 1965. "The relation of aggressive to sexual motivation." *Jour.Person.,* 33:462–475.

Barland, G.H. & D.C. Raskin. 1976. *Validity and Reliability of Polygraph Examinations of Criminal Suspects.* U.S. Dep't. of Justice Report #76-1. Salt Lake City: Department of Psychology, University of Utah.

Barndt, R.J. & D.M. Johnson. 1955. "Time orientation in delinquents." *Jour.Ab.Soc.Psych.,* 51:343–345.

Barron, J. 1974. *KGB: The Secret Work of Soviet Secret Agents.* New York: Bantam Books.

Barrow, R.L. 1975. "Fairness doctrine: A double standard for electronic and print media." *Hastings Law Jour.,* 26:659–708.

Barzun, J. 1962. "In favor of capital punishment." *Amer.Scholar,* 31:181–191.

Bauer, P.T. & J. O'Sullivan. 1977. "Ordering the world about: The new international economic order." *Policy Rev.,* 1:55–69.

Bellow, S. 1970. *Mr. Sammler's Planet.* New York: Viking.

Belson, W.A. et al. 1975. *Juvenile Theft: The Causal Factors.* London: Harper & Row.

Bequai, A. 1978. *Computer Crime.* Toronto: Heath.

Bergmann, G. 1968. "Ideology." In M. Brodbeck (ed.), *Readings in the Philosophy of the Social Sciences.* New York: Macmillan.

Berkson, J. 1955. "Smoking and lung cancer, some observations on two recent reports." *Jour.Amer.Stat.Assoc.,* 53:28.

Berliner, J.S. 1961. "The situation of plant managers." In A. Inkeles & K. Geiger (eds.), *Soviet Society: A Book of Readings.* Boston: Houghton, Mifflin.

Bethell, T. 1980b. "The Soviet sphere of influenza." *Amer.Spectator,* 13:5–6.

Bierce, A. 1958. *The Devil's Dictionary.* New York: Dover.

Blankenburg, E. 1976. "The selectivity of legal sanctions: An empirical investigation of shoplifting." *Law & Soc.Rev.,* 11:109–130.

Blasi, A. 1980. "Bridging moral cognition and moral action: A critical review of the literature." *Psych.Bull.,* 88:1–45.

Blenkner, M. 1954. "Predictive factors in the initial interview in family casework." *Soc.Service Rev.,* 28:65–73.

Bloom, L. & R. Riemer. 1949. *Removal and Return: The Socio-Economic Effects of the War on Japanese Americans.* Los Angeles: Univ.Calif.Press.

Bloom, R.F. & E.G. Brundage. 1947. "Prediction of success in elementary schools for enlisted personnel." In D.B. Stuit (ed.), *Personnel Research and Test Development in the Bureau of Naval Personnel.* Princeton, N.J.: Princeton U.P.

Bok, S. 1978. *Lying: A Moral Choice in Public and Private Life.* New York: Pantheon.

Boyle, A. 1979. *The Climate of Treason.* London: Hutchinson.

Braucht, G.N. et al. 1980. "Victims of violent death: A critical review." *Psych.Bull.,* 87:309–333.

Brzezinski, Z. 1969. "Five years after Kruschchev." *Survey,* #72:39.

Buchanan, J.M. et al. 1978. *The Consequences of Mr. Keynes.* London: Institute of Economic Affairs.

Buchanan, J.M. & R.E. Wagner. 1977. *Democracy in Deficit: The Political Legacy of Lord Keynes.* New York: Academic Press.

Bulkeley, W.M. 1979. "To some at Harvard telling lies becomes a matter of course." *Wall St.Jour.,* 100:1, 32 (Jan. 15).

Burlingame, R. 1954. *Henry Ford.* New York: New American Library.

Burton, R.V. 1963. "Generality of honesty reconsidered." *Psych.Rev.,* 70:481–499.

Caen, H. 1978. "In this corner." *The San Francisco Chronicle*, 19 (Aug. 28).

Calzón, F. 1978. "Castro and the peasants." *Nat.Rev.*, 30:1418–1419 (Nov. 10).

Cameron, M.O. 1964. *The Booster and the Snitch: Department Store Shoplifting.* Glencoe, Ill.: Free Press.

Camp, G. 1967. *Nothing to Lose: A Study of Bank Robbery in America.* Ph.D. dissertation. New Haven: Yale University.

Canadian Press. 1978b. "Curse triggered arson blazes." (Dec. 15).

Carney, L.P. 1980. *Corrections: Treatment and Philosophy.* Englewood Cliffs, N.J.: Prentice-Hall.

Carroll, J.S. 1978. "A psychological approach to deterrence: The evaluation of crime opportunities." *Jour.Person.Soc.Psych.*, 36:1512–1520.

Castro, F. 1971. Farewell speech, Chile. *U.S. News & World Report*, 71:76 (Dec. 20).

Cattell, R.B. 1980. *Personality and Learning Theory. Vol. 2: A Systems Theory of Maturation and Structured Learning.* New York: Springer.

Chalidze, V. 1977. *Criminal Russia: Essays on Crime in the Soviet Union.* Trans. by P.S. Falla. New York: Random House.

Ching, F. 1980. "China's legendary farming commune falsified output, People's Daily says." *Wall St. Jour.*, 103:26 (July 8).

Chou, S-h. 1963. *The Chinese Inflation, 1937–1947.* New York: Columbia U.P.

Clinard, M. 1954. Review of Cressey, "Other People's Money." *Amer.Sociol.Rev.*, 19:362.

Cobb, R. 1980. "The bad boy from Clichy." *Times Lit.Suppl.*, #4024:515 (May 9).

Cohen, J.A. 1968. *The Criminal Process in the People's Republic of China: 1949–1963.* Cambridge, Mass.: Harvard U.P.

——. 1977. "Reflections on the criminal process in China." *Jour.Crim.Law & Crim.*, 68:323–355.

Cohen, L.E. & M. Felson. 1979. "Social change and crime rate trends: A routine activity approach." *Amer.Sociol.Rev.*, 44:588–608.

Cohen, L.E., M. Felson, & K.C. Land. 1980. "Property crime rates in the United States: A macrodynamic analysis, 1947–1977, with ex ante forecasts for the mid-1980s." *Amer.Jour.Sociol.*, 86:90–118.

Connor, W.D. 1972. *Deviance in Soviet Society: Crime, Delinquency, and Alcoholism.* New York: Columbia U.P.

Cooney, J.E. 1979. "Cuban clan: The Garcias of Havana strongly back Castro despite the problems." *Wall St.Jour.*, 101:1,7 (Dec. 31).

Crain, W.M. & R.B. Ekelund. 1978. "Deficits and democracy." *Southern Econ.Jour.,* 44:813–828.

Cressey, D.R. 1953. *Other People's Money: A Study in the Social Psychology of Embezzlement.* Glencoe, Ill.: Free Press. 2nd ed., 1971. Belmont, Calif.: Wadsworth.

——. 1964. "Causes of employee dishonesty." Paper presented at the Top Management Business Security Seminar. East Lansing, Mich. (Apr. 16).

Davids, A. & B.B. Falkof. 1975. "Juvenile delinquents then and now: Comparison of findings from 1959 and 1974." *Jour.Ab.Psych.,* 84:161–164.

Davidson, J.D. 1980. *The Squeeze.* New York: Summit Books.

Davis, A. 1970. "Her revolutionary voice cries damnation of the system." *Life,* 69:26–27 (Sept. 11).

Deloatch, B. & S. Roach. 1977. *Crime in Service Industries.* Washington, D.C. U.S. GPO.

De Vany, A.S. et al. 1980. *A Property System Approach to the Electromagnetic Spectrum: A Legal-Economic-Engineering Study.* San Francisco: Cato Institute.

Devlin, P. 1965. *The Enforcement of Morals.* London: Oxford U.P.

Didion, J. 1978. "On morality." In her *Slouching Towards Bethlehem.* New York: Dell.

Dirks, R.L. & L. Gross. 1974. *The Great Wall Street Scandal.* New York: McGraw-Hill.

Donnerstein, E. 1980. "Aggressive erotica and violence against women." *Jour.Person.Soc.Psych.,* 39:269–277.

Drucker, P.F. 1980. "Toward the next economics." *Pub.Int.,* Special issue: 4–18.

Dudley, R.C. 1977. Personal correspondence. (Jan. 7).

Dunlap, J.W. & M.J. Wantman. 1944. *An Investigation of the Interview as a Technique for Selecting Aircraft Pilots.* Civil Aeronautics Administration Report #33. Washington, D.C.: C.A.A.

Dunlap, K. 1927. "The role of eye-muscles and mouth-muscles in the expression of emotions." *Genet.Psych.Monogs.,* 2:196–233.

Dunn, D.H. 1975. *Ponzi! The Boston Swindler.* New York: McGraw-Hill.

Dunne, F.P. 1901. *Mr. Dooley's Opinions.* New York: Russel.

Dworkin, R.H. et al. 1977. "Genetic influences on the organization and development of personality." *Develop.Psych.,* 13:164–165.

Economist. 1981. "How they made off with $21 million from the Wells Fargo stage." 278:77–78 (Feb. 28).

Einhorn, H.J. & R.M. Hogarth. 1978. "Confidence in judgment: Persistence of the illusion of validity." *Psych.Rev.,* 85:395–416.

Ekman, P. & W.V. Friesen. 1969. "Nonverbal leakage and clues to deception." *Psychiat.,* 32:88–106.

———. 1975. *Unmasking the Face.* Englewood Cliffs, N.J.: Prentice-Hall.

Ellul, J. 1965. *Propaganda: The Formation of Men's Attitudes.* New York: Random House.

Epstein, S. 1979. "The stability of behavior. I: On predicting most of the people much of the time." *Jour.Person.Soc.Psych.,* 37:1097–1126.

———. 1980. "The stability of behavior. II: Implications for psychological research." *Amer.Psych.,* 35:790–806.

Evola, J. 1930. *Fenomenologia dell'Individuo Assoluto.* Torino: Bocca.

———. 1934. *Rivolta contro il Mondo Moderno.* Milano: Hoepli.

Farnsworth, P.R. 1937. "Changes in attitudes toward men during college years." *Jour.Soc.Psych.,* 8:274–279.

Farran, R. 1981. "That noise from the closet caused by our old skeletons." *Edmonton Jour.,* p. A-8 (July 22).

Feldman, R.E. 1968. "Response to compatriot and foreigner who seek assistance." *Jour.Person. Soc.Psych.,* 10:202–214.

Fiedler, L. 1951. "Hiss, Chambers, and the age of innocence." *Commentary,* 12:109–119.

Fisher, F.M. & D. Nagin. 1978. "On the feasibility of identifying the crime function in a simultaneous model of crime rates and sanction levels." In A. Blumstein et al. (eds.), *Deterrence and Incapacitation: Estimating the Effects of Criminal Sanctions on Crime Rates.* Washington, D.C.: National Academy of Sciences.

Flew, A. 1976. "The profit motive." *Ethics,* 86:312–322.

Fly, J.W. & G.R. Reinhart. 1980. "Racial separation during the 1970s: The case of Birmingham." *Soc.Forces,* 58:1255–1262.

Franklin, C. 1967. *The Great Spies.* New York: Hart.

Fredlund, M.C. 1975. "The economics of animal systems." In G. Tullock (ed.), *Frontiers of Economics.* Blacksburg, Va.: University Publications.

———. 1975. "The economics of animal systems." In G. Tullock (ed.), *Frontiers of Economics.* Blacksburg, Va.: University Publications.

Friedan, B. 1973. Cited by *Newsweek,* 81:63 (May 14).

Fry, P.S. 1975. "Affect and resistance to temptation." *Develop.Psych.,* 11:466–472.

———. 1977. "Success, failure, and resistance to temptation." *Develop.Psych.,* 13:519–520.

Fuller, L.L. 1964. *The Morality of Law.* New Haven: Yale U.P.

Furman, W. & J.C. Masters. 1980. "Peer interactions, sociometric status, and resistance to deviation in young children." *Develop.Psych.,* 16: 229–236.

Gaither, G. 1961. *Consumer Motivation Research in Latin American and Other Countries.* Paper read at a meeting of the Personnel and Industrial Relations Association, Mexico City.

Ganzer, V.J. & I.G. Sarason. 1973. "Variables associated with recidivism among juvenile delinquents." *Jour.Consult.Clin.Psych.,* 40:1–5.

Geis, G. & E. Stotland (eds.). 1980. *White-Collar Crime: Theory and Research.* Beverly Hills: Sage.

Gendreau, P. & R.R. Ross. 1980. *Correctional Potency: Treatment and Deterrence on Trial.* Unpublished ms. Burritt's Rapids, Ontario: Rideau Correctional Centre, and Ottawa: University of Ottawa.

Gibbs, J.P. 1966. "Sanctions." *Soc.Probs.,* 14:147–159.

Glazer, N. & D.P. Moynihan (eds.). 1975. *Ethnicity: Theory and Experience.* Cambridge, Mass.: Harvard U.P.

Goldberg, L.R. & L.G. Rorer. 1965. *Learning Clinical Inference: The Results of Intensive Training on Clinicians' Ability to Diagnose Psychosis vs. Neurosis from the MMPI.* Paper presented at the meeting of the Western Psychological Association, Honolulu.

Graham, H.D. & T.R. Gurr. 1969. *Violence in America: Historical and Comparative Perspectives: A Report to the National Commission on the Causes and Prevention of Violence.* Washington, D.C.: U.S. GPO.

Graves, W.F. 1964. "The deterrent effect of capital punishment in California." In H. Bedau (ed.), *The Death Penalty in America.* Garden City, N.Y.: Doubleday.

Greenberg, D.F. n. d. (ca. 1979). *Mathematical Criminology.* New Brunswick, N.J.: Rutgers U.P.

Greenberg, D.F. et al 1979. "A panel model of crime rates and arrest rates." *Amer.Sociol.Rev.,* 44:843–850.

Greene, R. 1980. "You can't fight city hall—if you can't understand it." *Forbes,* 125:92–96 (Mar. 3).

Gregor, A.J. 1974. *The Fascist Persuasion in Radical Politics.* Princeton: Princeton U.P.

Groseclose, E. 1967. *Money and Man: A Survey of Monetary Experience.* New York: Ungar.

Guicciardini, F. 1965. *Maxims and Reflections of a Renaissance Statesman.* Trans. by M. Domandi. New York: Harper & Row.

Gur, R.C. & H.A. Sackeim. 1979. "Self-deception: A concept in search of a phenomenon." *Jour.Person.Soc.Psych.,* 37:147–169.

Guyon, J. 1980. "Hunt for wild boars is barred to hunters, but reporter joins it." *Wall St.Jour.,* 103:1, 8 (July 14).

Gwayne, J. 1980. Interview with Terry Campbell, "Stereo Morning," CBC-FM (July 18).

Hagan, J.L. 1971. *Psychologies Exposed: The Unexamined Psychological Premises of a Popular Explanatory Mode in "Deviance."* M.A. thesis. Edmonton: Department of Sociology, University of Alberta.

Hailsham, Lord of St. Marylebone. 1976. *Halsbury's Laws of England,* 4th ed. London: Butterworths.

Hall, G.S. 1890. "Children's lies." *Amer.Jour.Psych.,* 3:59–70.

Hall, J. 1947. *Principles of Criminal Law.* Indianapolis: Bobbs-Merrill.

Hamilton, W.H. & I. Till. 1942. "Property." In E.R.A. Seligman & A. Johnson (eds.), *Encyclopedia of the Social Sciences.* New York: Macmillan.

Hammond, K.R. et al. 1973. "Negative effects of outcome-feedback on multiple-cue probability learning." *Organiz.Beh. & Hum.Performance,* 9:30–34.

Harbin, G. 1979. "Hands off." *Sports Illus.,* 50:8 (Jan. 8).

Hardin, G. 1968. "The tragedy of the commons." *Science,* 162:1243–1248 (Dec. 13).

——. 1973. *Stalking the Wild Taboo.* Los Altos, Calif.: Kaufmann.

Hart, H.L.A. 1965. *The Morality of the Criminal Law.* London: Oxford U.P.

Hartshorne, H. & M.A. May. 1928–1930. *Studies in the Nature of Character.* 3 vols. New York: Macmillan.

Heineke, J.M. (ed.). 1978a. *Economic Models of Criminal Behavior.* New York: North-Holland.

——. 1978b. "Substitution among crimes and the question of deterrence: An indirect utility function approach to the supply of legal and illegal activity." In J.M. Heineke (ed.), *Economic Models of Criminal Behavior.* New York: North-Holland.

Hess, E.H. 1965. "Attitude and pupil size." *Sci.Amer.,* 216:46–54.

Hilgard, E.R. 1949. "Human motives and the concept of self." *Amer.Psych.,* 4:374–382.

——. 1977. *Divided Consciousness: Multiple Controls in Human Thought and Action.* New York: Wiley.

Hindelang, M.J. et al. 1978. *Victims of Personal Crime: An Empirical Foundation for a Theory of Personal Victimization.* Cambridge, Mass.: Ballinger.

Hinsie, L.E. & R.J. Campbell. 1960. *Psychiatric Dictionary.* 3rd ed. New York: Oxford U.P.

Hirschfeld, M. 1956. *Sexual Anomalies: The Origins, Nature, and Treatment of Sexual Disorders.* New York: Emerson Books.

Hirschi, T. & M.J. Hindelang. 1977. "Intelligence and delinquency: A revisionist review." *Amer.Sociol.Rev.,* 42:571–587.

——. 1978. "Reply to Ronald Simons." *Amer.Sociol.Rev.,* 43:610–613.

Holden, C. 1980. "Innovation: Japan races ahead as U.S. falters," *Science,* 210:751–754 (Nov. 14).

Hook, S. 1978. "A historian's verdict: The case of Alger Hiss." *Encounter,* 51:48–55.

Hooper, B. 1980. "Upstairs/Downstairs in 'New China'." *Encounter,* 54:13–20.

Hopkins, A. 1980. "Controlling corporate deviance." *Criminol.,* 18:198–214.

Hornung, E.W. 1969. *The Amateur Cracksman.* (Reprint of 1899 ed.). Freeport, N.Y.: Books for Libraries Press.

Horvath, F.S. 1977. "The effect of selected variables on interpretation of polygraph records." *Jour.Appl.Psych.,* 62:127–136.

Howells, T.H. 1938. "A study of ability to recognize faces." *Jour.Ab.Soc.Psych.,* 33:124–127.

Hughes, N.M. 1974. "Shoplifting statistics." *Security World,* 11:58–60.

Hume, D. 1955. *An Inquiry Concerning Human Understanding.* New York: Liberal Arts Press.

Jackson, P. 1981. "Rings of spies encircle the globe." *Edmonton Journal,* p. G-2 (July 18).

James, W. 1907. *Pragmatism.* New York: Longmans, Green.

Jaspan, N. 1960. *The Thief in the White Collar.* Philadelphia: Lippincott.

——. 1970. Interview. *U.S. News & World Report,* 69:32–33 (Oct. 26).

Jastram, R. 1977. *The Golden Constant: The English and American Experience, 1560–1976.* New York: Wiley.

Jensen, G.F. et al. 1978. "Perceived risk of punishment and self-reported delinquency." *Soc.Forces,* 57:57–78.

Johnson, W.O. 1978. "Daring young man on a tower of ice." *Sports Illus.,* 49:94–108.

Jones, D.A. 1979. *Crime Without Punishment.* Lexington, Mass.: Lexington Books.

Kamin, L.J. 1974. *The Science and Politics of IQ.* Potomac, Md.: Erlbaum.

Kaplan, H.B. 1976. "Self-attitudes and deviant response." *Soc.Forces,* 54:788–801.

Kelly, D.H. & W.T. Pink. 1973. "School commitment, youth rebellion, and delinquency." *Crim.,* 10:473–485.

Kelly, E.L. & D.W. Fiske. 1950. "The prediction of success in the V.A. training program in clinical psychology." *Amer.Psych.,* 5:395–406.

Kesey, K. 1964. *One Flew Over the Cuckoo's Nest.* New York: Compass Books.

Kinsey, A.C. et al. 1948. *Sexual Behavior in the Human Male.* Philadelphia: Saunders.

———. 1953. *Sexual Behavior in the Human Female,* Philadelphia: Saunders.

Kipnis, D. 1968. "Studies in character structure." *Jour.Person.Soc. Psych.,* 8:217–227.

Kirkwood, L. 1977. Unpublished report. Los Angeles: Security Consultants.

Koch, E.I. 1980. "The mandate millstone." *Pub.Int.,* #61:42–57.

Koch, S. 1974. "Psychology as science." In S.C. Brown (ed), *Philosophy of Psychology.* London: Macmillan.

Krafft-Ebing, R. von. 1935. *Psychopathia Sexualis: With Especial Reference to the Antipathic Sexual Instinct: A Medico-Forensic Study.* New York: Physicians & Surgeons Book Co.

Krauss, L.I. & A. MacGahan. 1979. *Computer Fraud and Countermeasures.* Englewood Cliffs, N.J.: Prentice-Hall.

Kraut, R.E. 1976. "Deterrent and definitional influences on shoplifting." *Soc.Probs.,* 23:358–368.

Krebs, R.L. 1968. *Some Relationships Between Moral Judgment, Attention, and Resistance to Temptation.* Ph.D. dissertation. Chicago: Department of Psychology, University of Chicago.

Kruse, V. 1953. *The Right of Property.* 2nd ed. London: Oxford U.P.

Lancaster, H. & G.C. Hill. 1981. "Anatomy of a scam: Fraud at Wells Fargo depended on avoiding computer's red flags." *Wall St.Jour.,* 104:1, 20 (Feb. 26).

Lane, H.L. 1977. *The Wild Boy of Aveyron.* London: Allen & Unwin.

Leff, A.A. 1976. *Swindling and Selling: The Story of Legal and Illegal Congames.* New York: Free Press.

Lehrman, L.E. 1980. "Real money." *Harper's Magazine,* 261:16–20.

Leng, S-c. 1977. "The role of law in the People's Republic of China as reflecting Mao Tse-tung's influence." *Jour.Crim.Law & Crim.,* 68:356–373.

Lickona, T. (ed.). 1976. *Moral Development and Behavior.* New York: Holt, Rinehart, Winston.

Lindesmith, A.R. 1965. *The Addict and the Law.* Bloomington, Ind.: Indiana U.P.

Lindsay, A.D. 1932. "Individualism." In E.R.A. Seligman & A. Johnson (eds.), *Encyclopedia of the Social Sciences.* New York: Macmillan.

Loftus, E.F. 1976. "Federal regulations: Make the punishment fit the crime." *Science,* 191:670 (Feb. 13).

Ludwig, A.M. 1965. *The Importance of Lying.* Springfield, Ill.: Thomas.

Lykken, D.T. 1974. "Psychology and the lie detector industry." *Amer.Psych.,* 29:725–739.

——. 1979. "The detection of deception." *Psych.Bull.,* 86:47–53.

——. 1980. "Polygraphic interrogation: The applied psychophysiologist." In A. Gale & J. Edwards (eds.), *Physiological Correlates of Human Behavior.* London: Academic Press.

——. 1981. *A Tremor in the Blood: Uses and Abuses of the Lie Detector.* New York: McGraw-Hill.

Lynn, R. 1961. "Introversion-extraversion differences in judgments of time." *Jour.Ab.Soc.Psych.,* 63:457–458.

Machiavelli, N. 1513. *The Prince.* Trans. by G. Bull, 1961. Middlesex, Eng.: Penguin Books.

——. 1584. "Discourses on the First Ten Books of Titus Livius." In P. Bondanella & M. Musa (eds.), *The Portable Machiavelli,* 1970, 1979. New York: Penguin Books.

Mack, J.A. 1972. "The able criminal." *Br.Jour.Crim.,* 12:44–54.

Mack, J.A. & H-J Kerner. 1975. "Le crime professionel et l'organisation criminelle." Lecture. Paris: University of Paris (May 20).

Marcuse, H. 1964. *One-Dimensional Man.* Boston: Beacon Press.

Martin, J.C. & I. Cartwright (eds.) 1978. *Martin's Annual Criminal Code.* Agincourt, Ont.: Canada Law Books.

Marton, K. 1979. "Hungary: The other side of the fence." *Atlantic Monthly,* 243:6–16.

Matthews, M. 1981. *Privilege in the Soviet Union.* London: Allen & Unwin.

Maxwell, N. 1972. "Passing judgment: How little town reacts when banker is accused of taking $4.7 million." *Wall St.Jour.,* 84:1, 14 (Aug. 8).

——. 1973. "Voice of expreience: Lamar Hill, embezzler, says stealing is easy." *Wall St.Jour.,* 86:1, 12 (June 19).

McCauley, C. et al. 1980. "Stereotyping: From prejudice to prediction." *Psychological Bulletin,* 87:195–208.

McClintick, D. 1977. *Stealing from the Rich: The Home-Stake Oil Swindle.* New York: Evans.

McPheters, L.R. 1976. "Criminal behavior and the gains from crime." *Crim.,* 14:137–152.

Meehl, P.E. & S.R. Hathaway. 1946. "The K factor as a suppressor variable in the Minnesota Multiphasic Personality Inventory." *Jour.Appl.Psych.,* 30:525–564.

Merritt, C.B. & E.G. Fowler. 1948. "The pecuniary honesty of the public at large." *Jour.Ab.Soc.Psych.,* 43:90–93.

Mill, J.S. 1859. *On Liberty.* Reprinted 1964. New York: Dutton.

Mischel, T. 1974. "Understanding neurotic behavior: From 'mechanism' to 'intentionality'." In T. Mischel (ed.), *Understanding Other Persons.* Totowa, N.J.: Rowman & Littlefield.

Mitchell, B. 1967. *Law, Morality, and Religion in a Secular Society.* London: Oxford U.P.

Moore, B., Jr. 1972. *Reflections on the Causes of Human Misery and Upon Certain Proposals to Eliminate Them.* Boston: Beacon Press.

Moore, K. 1980. "How's this, Mrs. Mullory?" *Sports Illus.,* 53:16–29 (Aug. 11).

Morland, N., 1958. *Science in Crime Detection.* New York: Emerson.

Moss, H.A. & E.J. Susman. 1980. "Constancy and change in personality development." In O.G. Brim, Jr. & J. Kagan (eds.), *Constancy and Change in Human Development.* Cambridge, Mass.: Harvard U.P.

Mottershead, D. 1980. *Person Perception.* Unpublished paper. Edmonton: Department of Sociology, University of Alberta.

Moynahan, B. 1978. *Airport International.* London: Macmillan.

Moynihan, D.P. et al. 1965. *The Negro Family: The Case for National Action.* Washington, D.C.: U.S. GPO.

Murphy, G. 1979. "Insurance industry readies a computer system to battle increase in arson." *Wall St.Jour.,* 100:1 (Feb. 22).

Mussen, P.H. & N. Eisenberg-Berg. 1977. *Roots of Caring, Sharing, and Helping: The Development of Prosocial Behavior in Children.* San Francisco: Freeman.

Mussen, P.H. et al. 1970. "Honesty and altruism among pre-adolescents." *Develop.Psych.,* 3:169–194.

National Commission on the Causes and Prevention of Violence. 1969. *To Establish Justice, to Insure Domestic Tranquility: Final Report of the National Commission.* Washington, D.C.: U.S. GPO.

National Review. 1980a. "The week." 32:816 (July 11).

Nelsen, E.A. et al. 1969. "Sources of variance in behavioral measures of honesty in temptation situations: Methodological analysis." *Develop.Psych.,* 1:265–279.

Nesbitt, W. & S. Candlish. 1978. "Determinism and the ability to do otherwise." *Mind,* 87:415–420.

Nettler, G. 1957. "A measure of alienation." *Amer.Sociol.Rev.,* 22:670–677.

———. 1974. "Embezzlement without problems." *Br.Jour.Crim.,* 14:70–77.

———. 1978. *Explaining Crime.* 2nd ed. New York: McGraw-Hill.

Newman, J. 1973. *Famous Soviet Spies: The Kremlin's Secret Weapon.* Washington, D.C.: U.S. News & World Report.

Normandeau, A. 1971. "Some data on shoplifting in Montreal department stores." *Can.Jour.Crim. & Corrections,* 13:251–265.

Oettinger, A.G. 1980. "Information resources, knowledge, and power in the 21st century." *Science,* 209:191–198 (July 4).

Offer, D. et al. 1979. *Psychological World of the Juvenile Delinquent.* New York: Basic Books.

Papanek, J. 1979. "Now New Mexico feels the heat." *Sports Illus.,* 51:32–41 (Dec. 10).

Parker, B. 1977. "Business: Victims of crime." *Security Management,* 21:28–31.

Patrick, H. & H. Rosovsky (eds.). 1976. *Asia's New Giant.* Washington, D.C.: Brookings Institution.

Pearline, L.I. et al. 1967. "Unintended effects of parental aspirations: The case of children's cheating." *Amer.Jour.Sociol.,* 73:73–83.

Penn, S. 1973. "Black Watch Farms collapse investigated: Fraud, $3.2 million embezzlement alleged." *Wall St.Jour.,* 88:4 (June 1).

Petersilia, et al. 1978. *Criminal Careers of Habitual Felons.* Report to the National Institute of Law Enforcement and Criminal Justice. Washington, D.C.: U.S. GPO.

Phillips, J.C. & D.H. Kelly. 1979. "School failure and delinquency: Which causes which?" *Crim.,* 17:194–207.

Pilot, O.R. 1952. *The Atom Spies.* London: Putnam's Sons.

Pincher, C. 1981. *Their Trade Is Treachery.* London: Sidgwick & Jackson.

Podlesny, J.A. & D.C. Raskin. 1978. "Effectiveness of techniques and physiological measures in the detection of deception." *Psychophysiol.,* 15:344–359.

Pokorny, A.D. 1965. "A comparison of homicides in two cities." *Jour.Crim.Law, Crim., & Police Sci.,* 56:479–487.

Pope, C.E. 1977. *Crime-Specific Analysis: An Empirical Examination of Burglary Offender Characteristics.* Washington, D.C.: U.S. Department of Justice.

Rainwater, L. & W.L. Yancey. 1967. *The Moynihan Report and the Politics of Controversy.* Cambridge, Mass.: MIT Press.

Raskin, D.C. et al 1976. *Validity and Reliability of Detection of Deception.* Mimeog. Salt Lake City: Department of Psychology, University of Utah.

Redden, E. 1939. *Embezzlement: A Study of One Kind of Criminal Behavior, With Prediction Tables Based on Fidelity Insurance Records.* Ph.D. dissertation. Chicago: Department of Sociology, University of Chicago.

Reed, T.E. 1977. "Racial comparisons of alcohol metabolism: Background problems and results." *Alcoholism: Clin.Exper.Res.,* 2:83–87.

Reid, D. 1979. "There's the devil to pay." *Sports Illus.,* 51:26–29 (Oct. 29).

Reppetto, T.A. 1974. *Residential Crime.* Cambridge, Mass.: Ballinger.

Rettig, S. & B. Pasamanick. 1964. "Differential judgment of ethical risk by cheaters and noncheaters." *Jour.Ab.Soc.Psych.,* 69:109–113.

Rife, D.C. 1948. "Genetic variability within a student population." *Amer.Jour.Phys.Anthro.,* 6:47–62.

Riis, R.W. 1941a. "The repair man will gyp you if you don't watch out." *Reader's Digest,* 39:1–6.

——. 1941b. "The radio repair man will gyp you if you don't watch out." *Reader's Digest,* 39:6–13.

——. 1941c. "The watch repair man will gyp you if you don't watch out." *Reader's Digest,* 39:10–12.

Roberts, A.H. et al. 1974. "Demographic variables, base rates, and personality characteristics associated with recidivism in male delinquents." *Jour.Consult.Clin.Psych.,* 42:833–841.

Robinson, W.S. 1951. "The logical structure of analytic induction." *Amer.Sociol.Rev.,* 16:812–818.

Rojek, D.G. 1979. "Private justice systems and crime reporting." *Crim.,* 17:100–111.

Ross, H.L. et al. 1970. "Determining the social effects of a legal reform: The British 'breathalyser' crackdown of 1967." *Amer.Beh.Sci.,* 13:493–509.

Ross, Irwin. 1980. "How lawless are big companies?" *Fortune,* 102:56–64 (Dec. 1).

Rubin, P.H. 1980. "The economics of crime." In R. Andreano & J.J. Siegfried (eds.), *The Economics of Crime.* New York: Wiley.

Russell, F. 1975. *A City in Terror.* New York: Viking.

Rutter, M. et al. 1964. "Temperamental characteristics in infancy and the later development of behavioural disorders." *Br.Jour.Psychiat.,* 110:651–661.

Sackeim, H.A. & R.C. Gur. 1979. "Self-deception, other-deception, and self-reported psychopathology." *Jour.Consult.Clin.Psych.,* 47:213–215.

Salem, R.G. & W.J. Bowers. 1970. "Severity of formal sanctions as a deterrent to deviant behavior." *Law & Soc.Rev.,* 5:21–40.

Salili, F. et al. 1976. "Achievement and morality: A cross-cultural analysis of causal attribution and evaluation." *Jour.Person.Soc.Psych.,* 33:327–337.

Sanders, C.R. 1975. "Caught in the con game: The young, white drug user's contact with the legal system." *Law & Soc.Rev.,* 9:197–218.

Schaie, K.W. & I.A. Parham. 1976. "Stability of adult personality traits: Fact or fable?" *Jour.Person.Soc.Psych.,* 34:146–158.

Schiffres, I.J. 1973. "Sedition, subversive activities, and treason." *Amer.Jurisprud.,* 70:1–32.

Schofield, C. 1980. *Mesrine: The Life and Death of a Supercrook.* London: Penguin.

Schuessler, K.F. 1954. Review of Cressey, "Other People's Money." *Amer.Jour.Sociol.,* 59:604.

Schur, E.M. 1965. *Crimes Without Victims: Deviant Behavior and Public Policy.* Englewood Cliffs, N.J.: Prentice-Hall.

Schwendinger, H. & J. Schwendinger. 1975. "Defenders of order or guardians of human rights?" In I. Taylor et al. (eds.), *Critical Criminology.* London: Routledge & Kegan Paul.

Seabury, P. 1980. "The third political lie." *Amer.Spectator,* 13:13–14.

Seligman, D. 1978. "Numbers game." *Fortune,* 98:36 (Dec. 4).

———. 1980. "Masochism in accounting." *Fortune,* 102:42 (Nov. 3).

Shils, E. 1975. *Center and Periphery: Essays in Macrosociology.* Chicago: Univ. Chicago Press.

Simon, C.K. 1978. "Crime—What punishment?" *Freedom at Issue,* #48:22–25.

Simon, W.E. 1978. *A Time for Truth.* New York: McGraw-Hill.

Smigel, E.O. & H.L. Ross (eds.). 1970. *Crimes Against Bureaucracy.* New York: Van Nostrand Reinhold.

Smith, J.C. & B. Hogan. 1973. *Criminal Law.* 3rd ed. London: Butterworths.

Smith, R.A. 1961. "The incredible electrical conspiracy." *Fortune,* 63:132–137, 161–164.

Sonnenfeld, J. & P.L. Lawrence. 1978. "Why do companies succumb to price fixing?" *Harvard Bus.Rev.,* 56:145–157.

Sorensen, R.C. 1973. *Adolescent Sexuality in Contemporary America: Personal Values and Sexual Behavior Ages Thirteen to Nineteen.* New York: World.

State of Indiana vs. Ford Motor Company. 1980. Cause # 11–431.

Stiegerwald, W. 1980. "Dictionary of the proletariat." *Amer.Spectator,* 13:47.

Stein, K.B. et al. 1968. "Future time perspective: Its relation to the socialization process and the delinquent role." *Jour.Consult.Clin. Psych.,* 32: 257–264.

Stekel, W. 1943. *Peculiarities of Behavior: Wandering Mania, Dipsomania, Kleptomania, Pyromania, and Allied Impusive Acts.* Trans. by J.S. Teslaar. New York: Liveright.

Stigler, G.J. 1970. "The optimum enforcement of laws." *Jour.Pol. Econ.,* 78:526–536.

Strong, E.K., Jr. 1962. "Nineteen year follow-up of engineer interests." *Jour.Appl.Psych.,* 36:65–74.

Sutherland, E.H. 1949. *White Collar Crime.* New York: Dryden.

Sutton, W. 1976. *Where the Money Was: The Memoirs of a Bank Robber.* (With E. Linn). New York: Viking.

Szucko, J.J. & B. Kleinmuntz. 1981. "Statistical versus clinical lie detection." *Amer.Psych.,* 36:488–496.

Tanner, T. 1965. "On Bellow's Herzog." *Encounter,* 24:58–70.

Tarlow, B. 1975. "Admissibility of polygraph evidence in 1975: An aid in determining credibility in a perjury-plagued system." *Hastings Law Jour.,* 26:917–974.

Taylor, R. 1967. "Causation." In P. Edwards (ed.), *The Encyclopedia of Philosophy.* New York: Macmillan.

Teresa, V. 1979. Interview, CBC-TV (Mar. 28).

Terman, L.M. 1938. *Psychological Factors in Marital Happiness.* New York: McGraw-Hill.

Thomas, A. et al. 1970. "The origin of personality." *Sci.Amer.,* 223:102–109.

Thurow, L.C. 1980. *The Zero Sum Society: Distribution and the Possibilities for Economic Change.* New York: Basic Books.

Tifft, L. & D. Sullivan. 1980. *The Struggle to Be Human: Crime, Criminology, and Anarchism.* Mt. Pleasant, Mich.: Cienfuegos Press.

Time. 1962. "Investigations: Decline and fall." 79:24–29 (May 25).

——. 1965. "Crime: The man who fooled everybody." 85:24–25 (June 4).

Toledano, Ralph de. 1977. *The Greatest Plot in History.* New Rochelle, N.Y.: Arlington.

Tufte, E.R. 1978. *Political Control of the Economy.* Princeton: Princeton U.P.

Tulchin, S.H. 1971. *Intelligence and Crime: A Study of Penitentiary and Reformatory Offenders.* Chicago: Univ. Chicago Press.

Turner, R.H. 1953. "The quest for universals in sociological research." *Amer.Sociol.Rev.,* 18:604–611.

Underwood, J. 1980. "Student athletes: The sham, the shame." *Sports Illus.,* 52:36–72 (May 19).

United States Comptroller General. 1978. *Arson-for-Profit: More Could Be Done to Reduce It.* Washington, D.C.: General Accounting Office.

Vandaele, W. 1978. "An econometric model of auto theft in the United States." In J.M. Heineke (ed.), *Economic Models of Criminal Behavior.* New York: North-Holland.

Vandivier, K. 1972. "The aircraft brake scandal." *Harper's Magazine,* 244:45–52.

Voltaire, F.M.A. 1764. *Dictionnaire Philosophique.* Trans. by P. Gay, 1962. New York: Basic Books.

Vreeland, R.G. & M.B. Waller. 1978. *Psychology of Firesetting: A Review and Appraisal.* Chapel Hill: Univ. North Carolina Press.

Wagner, R.E. & R.D. Tollison. 1980. *Balanced Budgets, Fiscal Responsibility, and the Constitution.* San Francisco: Cato Institute.

Wall Street Journal. 1973. "SEC accuses *Los Angeles Times* publisher, oil promoter, others in $30 million fraud." 88:5 (May 18).

———. 1980b. "Stilling the voice of Firestone." 103:28 (July 22).

———. 1980c. "Hurdles." 103:14 (Aug. 1).

———. 1980d. "Truth at Treasury." 103:28 (Aug. 19).

Waller, I. & N. Okihiro. 1978. *Burglary: The Victim and the Public.* Toronto: Univ. Toronto Press.

Wallis, W.A. 1976. *An Overgoverned Society.* New York: Free Press.

Ward, D.A. et al. 1969. "Crimes of violence by women." In D. Mulvihill et al (eds.), *Crimes of Violence.* Vol. 13. Washington, D.C.: U.S. GPO.

Warner, N.M. 1979. *Shoplifters in Bigstore.* M.A. thesis. Edmonton: Department of Sociology, University of Alberta.

Watt, R.M. 1963. *Dare Call It Treason.* New York: Simon & Schuster.

Weinberg, T.S. 1978. "Sadism and masochism: Sociological perspectives." *Bull.Amer.Aca. Psychiat. & Law,* 6:284–295.

Weinstein, A. 1978. *Perjury: The Hiss-Chambers Case.* New York: Knopf.

West, R. 1964. *The New Meaning of Treason.* New York: Viking.

Wiggins, N. & E.S. Kohen. 1971. "Man versus model of man revisited: The forecasting of graduate school success." *Jour.Person.Soc. Psych.,* 19:100–106.

Williams, G. 1958. *The Sanctity of Life and the Criminal Law.* London: Faber & Faber.

Williams, J.D. 1967. "Eager investors drop more than $50 million as debts outrun New Jersey bus operator." *Wall St.Jour.,* 77:1, 10 (Oct. 23).

Wilson, J.Q. & B. Boland. 1978. "The effect of the police on crime." *Law & Soc.Rev.,* 12:367–390.

Wilson, R.S. 1974. "Twins: Mental development in the pre-school years." *Develop.Psych.,* 10:580–588.

——. 1978. "Synchronies in mental development: An epigenetic perspective." *Science,* 202:939–948 (Dec. 1).

Wisher, C. 1974. "The teenage shoplifter." In M.M. Hughes (ed.), *Successful Retail Security.* Los Angeles: Security World.

Wolberg, L.R. 1948. *Medical Hypnosis.* 2 volumes. New York: Grune & Stratton.

Won, G. & G. Yamamoto. 1968. "Social structure and deviant behavior: A study of shoplifting." *Sociol. & Soc.Res.,* 53:44–55.

Yanowitch, M. 1981. *Social and Economic Inequality in the Soviet Union.* Armonk, N.Y.: Sharpe.

Yolton, J. 1973. "Action: Metaphysic and modality." *Amer.Phil.Quart.,* 10:71–85.

Young, R. 1973. "The historiographic and ideological contexts of the nineteenth-century debate on man's place in nature." In M. Teich & R. Young (eds.), *Changing Perspectives in the History of Science.* London: Heinemann.

Zahn, M. 1974. *Death by Murder: A Comparison Between Female Drug Users and Female Non-Users.* Paper read at the annual meeting of the Society for the Study of Social Problems. Montreal.

Zinn, H. 1967. "History as private enterprise." In K.H. Wolff & B. Moore (eds.), *The Critical Spirit.* Boston: Beacon Press.

Zito, T. 1980. "Why they call him 'Superthief'." *San Francisco Examiner & Chronicle,* pp. 2–3. (May 18).

Znaniecki, F. 1934. *The Method of Sociology.* New York: Rinehart.

NAME INDEX

Abramson, L.Y., 33
Adams, E., 51
Adams, J.R., 22
Adams, R, xi
Adler, A., 106
Andenaes, J., 115
Aronson, E., 19
Arrow, K.J., 23
Atrill, V., 91
Auletta, K., 22, 89, 90
Austin, R.L., 20
Ausubel, D.P., 72
Avison, W.R., xi

Bacon, D.C., 18
Baden, J., 62
Bailey, W.C., 116
Banfield, E.C., 32
Barber, R.M., 109
Barbu, Z., 14
Barclay, A.M., 98
Barland, G.H., 30
Barndt, R.J., 19
Barron, J., 44, 52, 56
Barrow, R.L., 8
Barzun, J., 102
Bastiat, F., 87
Bauer, P.T., 116
Bellow, S., 102
Belson, W.A., 16, 19, 101
Benning, J.S., 51
Bequai, A., 71

Bergmann, G., 46
Berliner, J.S., 22
Bethell, T., 22
Bierce, A., 18
Blake, G., 43
Blankenburg, E., 105, 106
Blasi, A., 20
Blenkner, M., 25
Bloom, R.F., 25
Blunt, A., 52, 54
Bok, S., 10
Boyer, R., 51
Boyle, A., 55
Brundage, E.G., 25
Brzezinski, Z., 47
Buchanan, J.M., 88
Bulkeley, W.M., 22
Burgess, G.F. deM., 54, 55, 59
Burton, R.V., 13, 20, 21

Caen, H., 108
Calzón, F., 22
Cameron, M.O., 104, 105
Camp, G., 114
Campbell, R.J., 105
Carney, L.P., 118
Carroll, J.S., 79
Carter, J., 92
Cartwright, I., 4, 38, 40, 65, 66
Castro, F., 92
Cattell, R.B., 50
Chalidze, V., 22

Chambers, W., 57, 58
Ching, F., 22
Chou, S-h., 89
Clinard, M., 72
Cobb, R., 100
Cohen, J.A., 22
Cohen, L.E., 21, 113
Connor, W.D., 118
Cooney, J.E., 22
Crain, W.M., 88
Cressey, D.R., 71, 72, 73, 74, 75, 76
Cuthbertson, E., 81

Davids, A., 19
Davidson, J.D., 89
Davis, A., 3
Deloatch, B., 107
Destutt de Tracy, A.L.C., 46
De Vany, A.S., 8
Devlin, P., 1
Didion, J., 37
Dirks, R.L., 80, 81, 83, 84
Donnerstein, E., 119
Drucker, P.F., 88
Drummond, N.C., 56
Dudley, R.C., xi
Dunlap, J.W., 25
Dunlap, K., 25
Dunn, D.H., 83
Dunne, F.P., 34
Dworkin, R.H., 119

Einhorn, J.H., 25
Eisenberg-Berg, N., 14
Eitzenberger, J., 52
Ekelund, R.B., 88
Ekman, P., 25
Ellul, J., 86
Epstein, S., 120
Evola, J., 49

Falkof, B.B., 19

Farran, R., 52
Feldman, R.E., 18, 21
Felson, M., 21, 113
Fiedler, L., 37
Fisher, F.M., 120
Fiske, D.W., 25
Flew, A., 49
Fly, J.W., 120
Fowler, E.G., 18
Franklin, C., 53
Fraser, J., xi
Fredlund, M.C., 120
Friedman, L.M., 62
Friesen, W.V., 25
Fry, P.S., 19
Fuchs, K., 53
Fuller, L.L., 1
Furman, W., 14, 19

Gaither, G., 23
Ganzer, V.J., 20
Geis, G., 6
Gendreau, P., 121
Glazer, N., 87
Goldberg, L.R., 29
Goldblum, S., 81, 82, 83, 84
Gouzenko, I., 52
Graham, H.D., 121
Greene, R., 22
Greenglass, D., 56
Greenwood, P.W., 102
Gregor, A.J., 47
Grim, P.F., 19
Groseclose, E., 88
Gross, L., 80, 81, 83, 84
Guicciardini, F., 86
Gur, R.C., 33
Gurr, T.R., 121
Guyon, J., 67
Gwayne, J., 8

Haber, R.N., 96
Hagan, J.L., 72

Hailsham, 39, 41
Hall, G.S., 21, 22
Hall, J., 1
Hamilton, W.H., 7
Hammond, K.R., 29
Harbin, G., 104
Hardin, G., 8, 62
Hart, H.L.A., 120
Hartshorne, H., 13, 19, 20, 21
Heineke, J.M., 113
Hess, E.H., 24
Hilgard, E.R., 24, 32, 33
Hill, G.C., 77
Hindelang, M.J., 20, 114
Hinsie, L.E., 105
Hirschfeld, M., 98
Hirschi, T., 20
Hiss, A., 36, 37
Hogan, B., 1
Hogarth, J., 25
Holden, C., 85
Hook, S., 58
Hooper, B., 22
Hornung, E.W., 111
Horvath, F.S., 30
Howells, T.H., 25
Hughes, N.M., 123
Hume, D., 18

Jackson, P., 52
James, W., 50
Jaspan, N., 107
Jastram, R., 88
Jensen, G.F., 123
Johnson, D.M., 19
Johnson, W.O., 98
Jones, D.A., 79
Joyce, W., 45, 47, 48

Kaplan, H.B., 19
Kelly, D.H., 19
Kerner, H-J., 109
Kesey, K., 70, 71

Kinsey, A.C., 98
Kipnis, D., 14, 19
Kirkwood, L., 103, 106, 107
Kleinmuntz, B., 29
Koch, E.I., 90
Kohen, E.J., 25
Krafft-Ebing, R. von., 98
Krauss, L.I., 77
Kraut, R.E., 105
Krebs, R.L., 20
Kruse, V., 62

Lancaster, H., 77
Land, K.C., 113
Lavin, M., 102
Lawrence, P.L., 86
Leff, A.A., 70
Lehrman, L.E., 88
Leng, S-c., 22
Lenin, N., 49
Lickona, T., 20
Lindsay, A.D., 62
Lott, R.P., 116
Ludwig, A.M., 10
Lunan, D.G., 51
Lykken, D.T., 24, 25, 27, 28, 30,
    31, 32

MacGahan, A., 77
Machiavelli, N., 86
Mack, J.A., 109, 110
Maclean, D., 53, 54, 58
MacLean, J.A., 110, 111
Marcuse, H., 50
Martin, J.C., 4, 38, 40, 65, 66
Marton, K., 22
Masters, J.C., 14, 19
Matthews, M., 49
Maxwell, N., 19, 75
May, A.N., 51
May, M.A., 13, 19, 20, 21
McCauley, C., 49
McCormick, G., 80

McPheters, L.R., 113
Meehl, P.E., 33
Merritt, C.B., 18
Mesrine, J., 99
Mettee, D.R., 19
Mill, J.S., 2
Minasian, J.R., 8
Mischel, T., 33
Mitchell, B., 1
Moore, B., Jr., 62
Moore, K., 22
Morland, N., 24, 31
Mosley, O., 47
Mottershead, D., 10
Moynahan, B., 107, 108
Moynihan, D.P., 87
Murphy, G., 67
Murphy, T.F., 58
Murray, H.A., 58
Mussen, P.H., 14, 19
Mussolini, B., 47

Nagin, D., 120
Nelsen, E.A., 14
Nettler, G., 2, 42, 74, 75, 89, 97, 113
Newman, J., 43, 52, 56
Nixon, R.M., 57
Norman, H., 52
Normandeau, A., 106

Oettinger, A.G., 8
Offer, D., 19
Okihiro, N., 108
Ortega y Gasset, J., 55
O'Sullivan, J., 116

Papanek, J., 22
Parham, I.A., 14
Parker, B., 107
Pasamanick, B., 19
Patrick, H., 85
Pearline, L.I., 22

Pearson, L., 52
Penn, S., 82
Petersilia, J.R., 102, 103
Philby, H.A.R., 54
Phillips, J.C., 19
Pilot, O.R., 56
Pincher, C., 52
Pink, W.T., 19
Platt, R., 81
Podlesny, J.A., 25
Pontecorvo, B., 53
Ponzi, C., 83
Pope, C.E., 109
Proudhon, P.J., 61

Raiffa, H., 22
Raskin, D.C., 25, 30
Redden, E., 76
Reid, D., 22
Reid, J., 30
Reinhart, G.W., 120
Reppetto, T.A., 108, 109
Rettig, S., 19
Riis, R.W., 17
Rinaldi, G., 52
Riordan, M., 81
Roach, S., 107
Roberts, A.H., 19
Robinson, W.S., 72
Rojek, D.G., 106
Roosevelt, E., 58
Rorer, L.G., 29
Rosenberg, E., 56
Rosenberg, J., 56
Rosovsky, H., 85
Ross, H.L., 19
Ross, I., 85
Ross, R.R., 121
Rubin, P.H., 78

Sackeim, H.C., 33
Sade, D.A.F. de., 67
Sanders, C.R., 129

Sarason, I.G., 20
Schaie, K.W., 14
Schiffres, I.J., 37, 38, 39, 40, 41, 42
Schofield, C., 99
Schuessler, K.F., 72
Schur, E.M., 2
Schwendinger, H., 3
Schwendinger, J., 3
Seabury, P., 12
Seligman, D., 92
Shils, E., 46
Shugar, 51
Silverman, R.A., xi
Simon, C.K., 129
Simon, W.E., 6, 91
Smigel, E.O., 19
Smith, D., 51
Smith, J.C., 1
Smith, R.A., 85
Sonnenfeld, J., 86
Sorensen, R.C., 98
Staub, H., 106
Steigerwald, W., 12
Stein, K.B., 19
Stekel, W., 106
St. John-Stevas, N., 1
Stotland, E., 6
Stroup, R., 62
Sudoplatov, P., 44
Sullivan, D., 62
Sutherland, E.H., 5, 72
Sutton, W., 96, 98, 99, 101
Szucko, J.J., 29

Tanner, T., 70
Tarlow, B., 31
Teresa, V., 96
Terman, L.M., 98
Thurow, L.C., 85
Tifft, L., 62
Till, I., 7

Toledano, R. de., 54
Tollison, R.D., 88
Tolstoy, L.N., 61
Tufte, E.R., 88
Tulchin, S.H., 20
Turner, R.H., 72

Uluschak, E., 90
Underwood, J., 22

Vandaele, W., 113
Vandivier, K., 84
Volokov, D., 52
Voltaire, F.M.A., 87
Vreeland, R.G., 67

Wagner, R.E., 88
Waller, I., 108
Waller, M.B., 67
Wallis, W.A., 6
Wantman, M.J., 25
Warner, N.M., 103, 104, 105, 106
Watkins, J., 52
Weinstein, A., 57, 58
Wennerström, S., 52
West, R., 45, 47
Whalen, W.H., 56
Wiggins, N., 25
Williams, G., 1
Williams, J.D., 132
Wisher, C., 105
Wolberg, L.R., 24
Won, G., 104, 106

Yamamoto, G., 104, 106
Yanowitch, M., 49
Young, R., 49

Zito, T., 110
Znaniecki, F., 72

SUBJECT INDEX

Alienation, 42, 45
Altruism, 59
Arbitrage, 83
Arson, 66–68
Authoritarianism, 46*n*–47*n*

Barratry, 4
Belief, 73
Bird-dog, 69
Burglary, 108–109

Cheating, 10, 80
Commons, tragedy of, 8, 62
Communism, 46, 46*n,* 48–50
Communist Party, 41
Con-games, 68–71
Cooler-outer, 70
Counterfeiting, 66
Crime:
    defined, 1
    victimless, 2*n*
    white-collar, 5–7
Cures, 71, 76–77

Deceit:
    and democracy, 86
    detection of, 23–31, 58
        by face, 25
        by guilty knowledge test, 27
        by lie control test, 26
        by perspiration, 24
        by polygraph, 26
        by truth control test, 26
        by voice strain, 28
    rational, 10, 84

Dishonesty:
    and competition, 21–22
    dimensions of, 9–12
    and failure, 19

Embezzlement:
    auditor's hypothesis, 74–75
    Canadian study of, 74
    Cressey's explanation, 71–74
    defined, 10, 64, 71
    detective's hypothesis, 74
    prescriptions for, 76–77
Epiphenomena, 100–101, 100n
Espionage, 40
Explanation and description, 100
Extortion, 63

False pretenses, 64
Fascism, 46n, 48
Forgery, 65
Fraud:
    by arson, 66
    in business, 78–79
    by con-games, 68–71
    by counterfeiting, 66
    by embezzlement, 64, 71
    by government, 83
    motives in, 80
    the Ponzi, 83, 87–94
    in politics, 11–12, 78–79, 87–94
    by propaganda, 86
    techniques, 82
    by uttering, 65

Guilt, 84n

Honesty:
    and competiton, 21–22
    contingencies of, 13–14, 19–23
    defined, 9
    distribution of, 14–19
    generality of, 13–14
    and IQ, 19–20
Hypnosis, 24

Idealism:
  as camouflage, 50
  motives of, 59
  and treason, 45
Ideas, 100–101
Ideology:
  Communist, 46, 46n, 48–50
  defined, 46, 48
  and temperament, 50, 99
Inflation, 88–89
Injury:
  concept of, 4–7
  by inflation, 87–89
  psychological, 4
  to social security, 4
  to social welfare, 5
  "victimless," 2n
Intentions:
  good and evil, 92–93
  and injuries, 89–92
Intimidation, 63

KGB, 55n
Kleptomania, 105

Leverage, 80
Liars:
  detection of, 23–31
  types of,
    pathological, 31
    psychopathic, 32
    self-deceivers, 32–33
Liberalism, 57n
Lying:
  defined, 9, 10
  and truth, 11
  utilities of, 9, 11–12

Mark, 69
Measurement:
  blind, 30n
  non-reactive, 20n
Minorities, 87, 106, 106n
Mischief, 63

Misprision, 39
Morality:
   meaning of, 36n
   "mouth," 20

Naziism, 46–47, 46n

Personality, 100
Polygraph, 26
Ponzi, 83
Profit motive, 49n, 49
Propaganda, 86, 86n
Property:
   concept of, 7–9, 61
   and personhood, 62
   persistence of, 62
Punishment, 112–113

Reality, 50
Reasons, 33n
Religion, 46n
Responsibility, 92
Robbery:
   concept of, 9n, 63
   by Mesrine, 97–98
   ordinary, 102–103
   by Sutton, 96–99
Roper, 69

Sabotage, 40
Sedition, 40–42
Shame, 84n
Shoplifting, 103–108
Societal engineering, 2n–3n
Stealing:
   contingencies of, 112–114
   cost-benefit schedule, 95
   defined, 10
   by employees, 107–108
   by force, 63
   by fraud, 63–92
   gain from, 101–112
   hostility in, 101–112

Raffles-type, 101–112
  satisfactions of, 96–99
  with talent, 109–112
Symbolic interaction, 73

Theft (*see* Stealing)
Totalitarianism, 46*n*–47*n*
Treason:
  accessories to, 39
  cases, 37–58
  and conscience, 37
  defined, 35–36, 37–39
  justifications of, 36
  misprision of, 39
  punishment of, 39
  recruitment to, 42–47
  warning signs, 58–59
Truth, 11

Vandalism, 63
"Verbal droppings," 59